• **Bartholomev**

WALK THE SOUTH DOWNS

by Anthony Burton

Bartholomew

A Division of HarperCollins*Publishers*

Published by Bartholomew, a Division of HarperCollins*Publishers*,
12 Duncan Street, Edinburgh EH9 1TA.

First published 1988
Reprinted 1989, 1991

© Bartholomew 1988

Printed in Great Britain by Bartholomew,
HarperCollins*Manufacturing*, Edinburgh.

Produced for Bartholomew by Curtis Garratt Limited,
The Old Vicarage, Horton cum Studley, Oxford OX9 1BT.
Typesetting and maps by Taurus Graphics.
Layouts by Burman Associates.

ISBN 0 7028 0811 3

CONTENTS

KEY MAP FOR THE WALKS

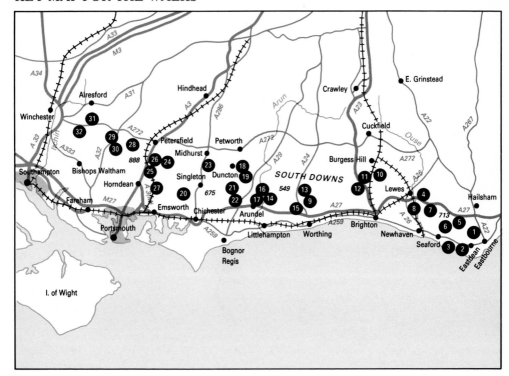

KEY TO SCALE AND MAP SYMBOLS

SCALE 1 : 63 360

SCALE 1 : 25 000

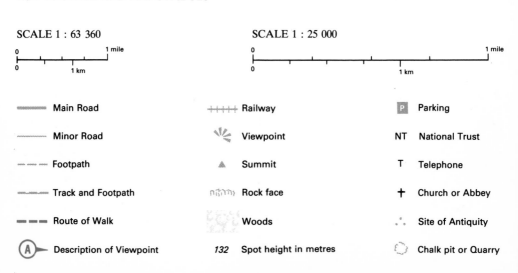

Main Road	Railway	P Parking
Minor Road	Viewpoint	NT National Trust
Footpath	Summit	T Telephone
Track and Footpath	Rock face	+ Church or Abbey
Route of Walk	Woods	.·. Site of Antiquity
A Description of Viewpoint	132 Spot height in metres	Chalk pit or Quarry

1 WALKING FOR PLEASURE

Some statistics have suggested that walking and country rambling have now ousted angling and gardening from being Britain's most popular leisure activities. Perhaps with the ever-increasing demands upon our countryside for roads, housing, industrial and agricultural land, and the generation of power, this is not entirely surprising. Environmental awareness among the public at large is also growing and, with the pressures put upon many people by modern lifestyles, escaping into the great outdoors when the chance arises becomes an important safety valve for many of us.

If all environmental doom-mongers were to be wholly believed, one might think that there was little wild or rural Britain left to escape into. This is certainly not the case and, even in the prosperous and built-up south-east, there is a wealth of glorious countryside to be enjoyed. It has to be admitted, though, that much of that countryside is the product of human endeavour, past and present. The South Downs and their immediate surroundings are within easy driving or railway distance of many major towns and cities, such as Portsmouth, Brighton, or even the metropolis of Greater London itself. Even so, there are quiet corners where rural peace and tranquillity can be found and where the only sounds to be heard are of insect or bird, farm dog or tractor, or simply the breezes rustling the treetops. At such moments, the bustling, car-packed streets and telephone-ringing offices of the urban centres seem many miles and many ages away.

The walks in this book have been specially selected to give a flavour of this part of south-eastern England, to represent the beauty and the variety of countryside to be found in a relatively small area, and also to show how the human factor does in no small way reflect the landscape itself whether in farming methods, past and present, the industries that have been pursued here, or the building materials that have been used. Most of the walks themselves are relatively easy to complete within an hour or two and, although the physical exercise they offer, is part of their value, it is not necessarily the most vital part. For those who look upon walking as a means of setting themselves physical or psychological challenges, then climbing the highest peaks in Scotland or completing a long-distance footpath, such as the Pennine Way, in record time may be more rewarding than a relaxing stroll among the woods and downlands of this part of England. But, even for those hardy souls, the softness of south-eastern countryside and the interest which the landscape presents may prove to be reward enough; at the very least, it is a chance to let the mind and body recover even from the demands of tough terrain.

It is possible, as the author well knows, to combine two or more of the walks in the book (sometimes by means of a short car journey) into a day's walking that many intrepid types would find gave their leg muscles a sense of achievement. This is not the book's purpose, however, (there are others that do that), but it is intended to guide the reader into one of England's most attractive stretches by means of quite gentle rambles that still offer plenty of interest to be seen, heard, or even smelt and touched!

2 ABOUT THE SOUTH DOWNS

The landscape of the Downs has been formed over a period that stretches back over millions of years. As far as the landscape we see today is concerned, the story begins when the whole region was covered with a vast, freshwater lake, the bed of which was made up of sands and clays. Then the sea broke through, bringing with it myriads of tiny shellfish. When they died, their bodies sank to the seabed where they decomposed leaving their hard skeletons behind, the white mass we know as chalk. Eventually, the sea receded, leaving a land where a layer of chalk sat above the soft sands and clays. After that came a period of great upheaval when the landmass buckled to form hills and ridges, valleys and depressions.

A great dome was formed stretching all the way from what we now call southern England to France. In time, this, too, was broken up. The sea swept through to form the English Channel, leaving just a part of the dome behind in England. After that the slow, inexorable forces of wind and rain began to eat into the chalk. The centre of the dome was destroyed, leaving the rest as two ridges with a deep depression between. This, in effect, is the landscape we see today: the two chalk ridges of the North and South Downs, separated by the plain of the Weald. That is the simple pattern, but the water collecting in the Weald needs its outlet to the sea, so river valleys can be found cutting through the ridge of chalk.

What does all this long history mean to walkers out for a stroll in this area? It does, in fact, dictate almost everything that is met along the way. The shape of the Downs, the rolling undulating landscape, is produced by the gentle weathering of the chalk. The steep, scarp face that marks the northern edge of the South Downs is simply the result of the collapse of the central portion of the once-extensive dome. The rivers that have forced their way through the ridge have created their own landscape of flat, marshy flood plains while, in the central, eroded area of the Weald, the weather has cut right through to expose ancient sands and clays. So, in walking the Weald you expect to find, and do find, a heavy, often soggy way to follow. On the uplands, in contrast, heavy use has bitten through the thin layer of turf to expose the chalk which provides a firm, sparkling-white path in dry weather but which can become a grey slither in the wet. The practical implication of this state of affairs is that the walker is well advised to be well shod for the great majority of these walks. Paths in the valley are always inclined to be muddy and, after heavy rain, can become quagmires. The upland paths remain generally firm but rain softens the chalk which sticks in unpleasant lumps to the feet. In such conditions, walking boots or properly designed walking shoes offer very great advantages. Good footwear is equally to be recommended for any walk which involves going up or down one of the steep scarp slopes, where it is all too easy for someone in flimsy footwear to turn an ankle or even suffer a more serious injury.

When one comes to look at the landscape in more detail, the underlying patterns still have a pronounced effect. The rivers that cut through from the eroded centre of the old dome have created wide flood plains, wildernesses of marshland that people have had to tame by an elaborate system of drainage channels and ditches, creating the characteristic chequerboard pattern of criss-cross lines that can be seen, for example, in the area of the Amberley Wild Brooks. The flat, river valleys also form the obvious transport routes for the area which, in turn, have given the breakthrough points in the chalk ridge a special strategic significance. It is at precisely these points that the most important towns and settlements are found.

Even more marked are the differences between the uplands of the chalk downs, and the clayey lowlands of the great bowl of the Weald. The former has a landscape of thin soil, which can only be made to support crops with a great deal of difficulty. At the eastern end of the Downs, the overlying soil is at its thinnest – and, just how thin that cover is, can be seen where the sea has broken through to create the tall, white cliffs of the Seven Sisters. So here, trees are, at best, poor stunted things and this, too, has implications for the walker. There is little cover from the sun – so, a sun hat is a useful item to have by you in good weather – and no cover from the rain, so that good, waterproof clothing is also invaluable. Down in the Weald, things are very different, for the clays once supported a vast area of forest, traces of which remain in isolated copses and more extensive areas of woodland. Here, there is shelter in plenty but the heavy soil can make for heavy going in the wet and, where individual walks are indicated as being especially bad, the warnings should be taken seriously. There is not much fun to be had in tramping up to your ankles in cloying mud.

3 PLANTS AND ANIMALS

The different habitats of the area – chalk upland, wooded, clayey Weald, and river flood plain – all have their own characteristic plants and animals. The upland Downs were, until quite recently, smooth, grass-covered hills, and had been for many centuries. They were mostly given over to grazing sheep and cattle and, in some parts, they still are. This makes for superb walking country, as you seem almost to bounce along on the springy turf that you can still find, for example, on the downs above Fulking or round Chanctonbury Ring.

Elsewhere, modern mechanized farming techniques and intensive use of fertilizers have brought the area under cultivation. This has resulted in a dearth of wild flowers and plants in those regions. But the phenomenon is not new. As far back as the

Stone Age, the downland was cultivated, simply because the thin soil provided less of an obstacle to the primitive ploughs than did the heavy clays of the Weald. But even before that, the Downs were covered by rough woodland and scrub that had to be cleared before cultivation could begin. Woodland does, in fact, become steadily denser as one travels westward along the Downs.

The thin, chalky soils of the uncultivated Downs have their own quite distinctive plant life, which give the special character to virtually all the walks in this book. There are three principal grasses that make up the turf: sheep's fescue, the tall, upright brome, and carnation sedge with its distinctive bluish-green leaves. Herbs thrive among the grasses, lending their scents to the hill air: salad burnet is common, and you can find such plants as selfheal, which was once used for treating cuts and wounds. There are many small flowers that thrive, such as milkwort, which can be blue, white, or pink, the brilliant yellow bird's-foot trefoil, and vetches. The true glory of the Downs are, however, the orchids which can still be found over wide areas of uncultivated land. The plants provide the attraction for a rich insect life and, in summer, butterflies are common, particularly the small heath and the beautiful chalkhill blue.

The one form of life that is always present and which leaves a lasting impression with any walker on the Downs is the bird life. The song of the skylark forms what can seem an almost continuous, and always beautiful, accompaniment to any walk on the uplands. The corn bunting, partridge, and quail offer rather less musical accompaniment, and the cuckoo regularly joins in the chorus. A common sight, hovering over the Downs, is the kestrel. The more heavily wooded sections to the west have their own inhabitants, such as the treecreeper and the nuthatch, while the staccato rattle of the woodpecker often echoes through the trees. Another common resident, often to be seen on the fringe of the woods or strutting at the edge of a cornfield is the pheasant. Of the remaining animal life, the rabbit is by far the commonest, but deer can also be seen, albeit briefly, at the edges of woods. Adders live in the downs, but should not be a cause for concern – they are as keen to avoid contact with walkers, as walkers are anxious to avoid them. The harmless slowworm is also occasionally seen.

The Weald at the base of the Downs offers a quite different range of life. Until recently, the glory of the lower ground were the hedgerows with their mixture of shrubs and trees and banks rich with flowers. Sadly, many of these have now been grubbed out to make way for the wide acres of modern farming. Where they survive, they are invariably bright with colour and rich in scent. Honesuckle, blackthorn, and dog rose look down on celandine, vetch, and campion. Elsewhere, one may be lucky enough to find meadows with the familiar buttercups, daisies, and dandelions, and the poppy seems to be coming back into ascendancy, so that it is possible to see whole fields of the brilliant red flowers stretched out at the foot of the Downs. Here, too, one finds the woodland still dominated by those great trees, the beech and the oak. Bushes frequently drip with travellers'-joy which, in autumn, hangs down in the grey feathery fronds that earn it the alternative name of old-man's-beard. The commonest bird cries are those of the woodpigeon, with its hollow, monotonous hoo-hoo-hooing. But any of the commoner British field birds can be expected to put in an appearance, while the river valleys can boast a fine mixture of waterfowl and seabirds strayed upriver from the coast. It would be impossible in such a brief introduction to do more than hint at the richness of plant and animal life to be met on these walks, but you can at least be assured that there will always be something to see or hear.

4 THE HISTORY OF THE DOWNS

The natural world represents only a part of the story of the Downs, for the landscape we see today would look very different if people had not intervened. Primitive man first appeared in this area 500 000 years ago, when the great chalk dome stretched unbroken from England to France, but these people had little or no impact on the landscape. The first important changes came with the Neolithic or New Stone Age which lasted from around 4000 to 2000 BC. On any walk on the Downs, you will see flint nodules lying on the ground. If you pick up one of the smaller flakes, you will find it has a sharp cutting edge.

Flint can be 'knapped', that is, large nodules can be broken down and shaped by skilful workmen to make all kinds of useful objects, from sharp axes to arrow heads and knives. These are the tools that give the Stone Age its name. The axes were quite good enough to clear the trees from the upland Downs, and the job could be finished off by burning. It is to these people of 5000 years ago that we owe the open scenery of the Downs that we all enjoy today. They have also left more specific features behind. The most obvious are the long barrows or burial mounds, which might once have contained as many as fifty bodies. A fine example is to be seen near the famous Long Man of Wilmington. Here, too – but much more obviously on Cissbury Hill – are the other characteristic reminders of Neolithic Man. Shallow hollows, surrounded by a raised ring of earth pockmark the ground. These were originally pits where men dug down to reach layers of flint beneath the surface, for people soon found that the best material was not to be found among the nodules lying around on the surface. So they excavated down to the flint and then tunnelled out, hacking away using deer antlers as pickaxes. In time the pits were abandoned and collapsed in, leaving the hollows we see today. These people traded their flints over a wide area, and the tracks they followd are the same tracks we walk for pleasure today.

The Stone Age gave way to the Bronze Age which left another characteristic feature on the downland landscape – the tumuli or round barrows, circular humps which, like the long barrows, were used for burial. The most spectacular examples are the Devil's Jumps, a line of five on the brow of Treyford Hill above Kingley Vale. When, however, we come to the Iron Age that began around 500 BC and continued to the time of the Roman settlement, we reach a period which has produced some of the most striking and distinctive of downland features – the hill forts.

In the really big fort, you find a regular pattern followed. The fort itself is generally a flat area at the top of the hill, and surrounding it are the defences of rampart and ditch, which would originally have been made even more formidable by the addition of wooden palisades. The sites were generally chosen to make maximum use of natural features, particularly high vantage points and steep slopes, so that the forts occupy all the most prominent positions met with along the length of the Downs. There are half a dozen really big and impressive forts along the way, and all are visited on different walks. It is not altogether clear whether these forts were, in effect, fortified villages or places which could be temporarily occupied in times of war. They certainly suggest a time when intertribal struggles and fights over land must have been common but, just occasionally, this downland landscape sends back a more peaceful message.

The people of the Iron Age cultivated the land. Their ploughs were not very efficient, but were quite good enough to cope with the thin soil of the uplands. They worked small fields on the sides of the hills and, with repeated ploughings, there was a tendency for the soil to pile up on the downhill side in distinct ridges, and, because the fields were often set at odd angles, these ridges formed on all four sides. They are known as 'lynchets', and they can be seen defining a typical group of fields in a very clear manner on the hillside above Jevington.

The Celtic tribes who built the hill forts and ploughed the Downs were eventually to be defeated in war by the invading armies of Rome. Roman remains are comparatively rare on the Downs, but those that are met along the way are at least plain to see and of considerable importance. The most obvious relic is Stane Street which ran from Chichester, Roman Regnum, to London. Many Roman roads only appear as the straight line of the modern road built over the same route, but Stane Street in its path across the Downs still retains the essential character of the original. The walk through Eartham Wood follows Stane Street for over a mile (2 km). Close to Stane Street are the very impressive remains of the Roman villa at Bignor, which lies very close to another of the walks and which is open to the public.

Of the long period of decline that followed the end of the Roman Empire, comparatively little is known, hence the popular name Dark Ages. There is certainly very little that one can point to in the landscape and say with any conviction – this belongs to that misty period of time. But things become clearer with the arrival of Christianity and the conversion of the Saxons, who had settled in Sussex at the end of the fifth century AD. Churches were built and, although most were replaced by later, and often grander, buildings over the centuries, a few still survive to give an impression of the level of sophistication of these people. Jevington church actually made use of Roman bricks and contains a Saxon carving. It is not, however, the church architecture that is most important here, but the siting of the churches. The hill forts of the Iron Age had given way to the villages of the valleys and the Weald. This represented a vital shift in emphasis. From this time, right through the Norman Conquest and on towards quite modern times, the use of the land was to be quite different from that of prehistory. The old, square fields scratched out of the uplands were abandoned as new, heavy ploughs came into use, capable of cutting through the heavy clays. If left quite alone, the Downs would soon have reverted to scrub and thicket, but the flocks of downland sheep steadily munched their way over the hills, keeping vegetation down to a smooth grassland. And, just as the fields were abandoned, so too were the upland settlements, and even now it is rare to find anything more than the occasional isolated farmstead along the downland ridge. Walkers on the Downs experience a feeling of great spaciousness thanks to this change in agriculture that began more than 1000 years ago.

5 DOWNLAND LANDSCAPE TODAY

The changing patterns of the centuries can be seen by walkers in two ways. Firstly, there are the long views, the wide panoramas that are such a feature of any walk along the tops. Then there are the more intimate close-ups seen when the walker comes down to the valley floor. So, let us start with the widest view and then go on to fill in the details. Even today, there is an overriding impression of a wooded area, and it is not difficult to see that this is a landscape where woodland has been cleared for farmland and settlement rather than a region where woods have been planted. Villages crop up at regular intervals all along the foot of the north-facing escarpment, and there is good reason for this. They are taking advantage of the freshwater springs that flow out from the chalk. These provided drinking water for the human inhabitants and a ready means of washing the downland sheep, so that their fleeces were ready for market. These springs are seen at their clearest at Fulking, where they flow out through elaborate ceramic surrounds, emblazoned with suitably improving biblical texts.

The other principal features appear where rivers have forced a way through the chalk ridge to reach the sea. These rivers formed the main highways of trade throughout those centuries when the roads of the Weald were little better than clayey tracks. They snake inland through the hills, and the end of the tideway is often marked by an important development. Towns such as Arundel and Lewes owe their importance to their roles as links between the interior of south-east England and the sea. Even the smaller towns, higher up the minor rivers, profited from their maritime connections. Alfriston on the Cuckmere grew rich on European trade, both licit and illicit, for it was a notorious haunt of smugglers. For many hundreds of years, transport by navigable river was cheaper than movement overland. This was especially true of the Weald, where the heavy clays made tracks all but impassable in wet seasons before the advent of surfaced roads.

Focusing more closely on the lowland landscape shows significant features. The most important settlements on the banks of the major rivers are heavily fortified. Arundel, for example, is centred on the great castle that guards the point where the River Arun breaks through the hills to make its way to the sea. It is no longer obvious why this should be a strategic centre, but that is only because modern development based on the motorcar has reduced the town to the status of a picturesque backwater. Once, it was quite different, with a busy wharf area and a brisk trade, improved in the eighteenth century by canal connections with London. It requires something of an act of imagination to see towns such as this as thriving ports, just as it seems difficult to envisage the narrow, winding rivers that link the Weald to the sea as major trading routes. Yet it is this importance of river communication that created all the major towns that one meets throughout the whole region.

Walking the area, patterns do begin to emerge, and it soon becomes a simple matter to determine why one village grew and another stagnated. But when one comes to look even more closely at the settlements, whether hamlets or large towns, other factors begin to assume significance. Building materials are the key to the special character of the downland settlements. Stone is not available locally, so builders have turned to other materials, the most obvious of which is timber. The timber-framed building deserves a treatise rather than a few lines, but it is as well to be aware of its essentials. Houses were built as empty boxes, a jigsaw of horizontal and vertical members. But everything was pre-fabricated, the members all cut to size and then assembled on site. All that was needed after that was a suitable material to plug the gap – wattle and daub in the oldest buildings, bricks in the more recent. Add a roof of thatch or tile and you have what was in its day a simple home, but which now seems the perfect picturesque landscape feature. Designers of more important structures, such as churches, were faced with a dilemma: to import building stone at great expense or to find a local alternative. The latter usually turned out to be flint. Nodules could be split to present a round, shiny black surface, and the flints could then be embedded in plaster to create a wall.

Other materials which catch the eye have equally local origins. The clays of the Weald are ideal for manufacturing bricks and tiles. So, the simple houses often have, as one might expect, tiles on the roof, but also have tiles hung on the walls to improve weather proofing. The other local material which adds to the character of the downland scene is thatch – and no material seems more at home in the English countryside than this. What we now see as colourful, picturesque villages turn out to be no more than local responses to local needs. Perhaps it is here that their charm lies, for the villages and towns belong to this particular region of England and to no other.

Development in the region did little to change the overall pattern until quite recently. The years after World War 2 have, however, produced a quite new landscape. The downland area devoted to grazing has steadily diminished to be replaced by fields of cereal crops. New machines and new chemical fertilizers have made it feasible, once again, to farm the uplands. This has certainly not made for a more attractive landscape, and it is ironical that these new farming developments have coincided with an increased interest in the leisure uses of the countryside. It was in 1947 that a Special Committee on Footpaths and Access to the Countryside recommended the establish-ment of six long-distance footpaths, the South Downs Way among them. The route was not, however, officially opened until 1972 but it is now established as a popular, well-used route for walkers – a route which appears time and again in the various walks described in this book. This is the latest of the many changes that have overtaken the countryside – its use for leisure. But that use depends, in good measure, on all that has gone before, through the centuries of historic development and even further back through prehistory to the almost unimagin-able eons of geological time. This very brief introduction is intended to provide a perspective to the walks that follow.

6 WALKING THE SOUTH DOWNS

Before moving on to the detailed des-criptions of the routes themselves, it seems appropriate to summarize the nature of the walks and the problems that walkers might expect to encounter. The first thing that should be stressed is that none of the walks is especially arduous. The only strenuous sections are those which involve a climb up the scarp face from the valley to the top of the Downs. So, the gradings which are attached to the walks should be seen in this context, and even those which are indicated as being particularly difficult will, at worst, make the average walker feel out of breath and heavy limbed for only part of the way. There is nothing exceptionally strenuous on offer, nor is there anything particularly dangerous – no crags or precipices to cause concern. Nevertheless, it is always wise to allow more time than might appear necessary at first glance, and to come prepared for bad weather because so many of the walks provide little in the way of shelter.

All the walks are on public footpaths and bridleways, which it is your right to use. It is the landowner's responsibility to ensure that gates and stiles are properly maintained and that paths are kept open. All these walks have been tested by the author, so you should not experience any difficulties, but it has to be left to the discretion of the individual whether to step boldly across a ploughed field or to take a more diplomatic route around the edge. It should, however, always be borne in mind that, on many occasions, you are walking across land on which someone depends for a livelihood, and every care should be taken to keep to official routes and to avoid causing unnecessary damage. Walkers will be doing no harm to local farmers, to other walkers, or even to themselves if they stick absolutely to the Country Code, as spelled out by the Countryside Commission:

1 Enjoy the countryside and respect its life and work.
2 Guard against all risks of fire.
3 Fasten all gates.
4 Keep your dogs under close control.
5 Keep to public paths across farmland.
6 Use gates and stiles to cross fences, hedges, and walls.
7 Leave livestock, crops, and machinery alone.
8 Take your litter home.
9 Help to keep all water clean.
10 Protect wildlife, plants, and trees.
11 Take special care on country roads.
12 Make no unnecessary noise.

Walk 1

COMBE HILL AND JEVINGTON

3 miles (4¾ km) Moderate

This is a pleasant, open walk, including sections of both the South Downs Way and the Weald Way. It begins at the delightful village of Jevington which is reached by a minor road that turns south off the A22 and passes through Wannock. Drive through Jevington and the car park is on the right, just past the Hungry Monk restaurant.

5 *Where the path divides, turn left through the woodland and immediately right following the yellow arrow.*

4 *Where the path divides, take the left fork and then turn immediately left again by the concrete sign, following the green path through the gorse bushes.*

6 *Cross the stile into the field, and take the path straight ahead.*

7 *Follow the road down past the houses and at the main road turn left to return to the start.*

Combe Hill

Neolithic Camp

Wealdway

Babylon Down

Jevington

Willingdon

South Downs Way

201

1 *From the car park, turn left up the road and right up the road marked South Downs Way.*

2 *At the top of the hill by a stone marked Eastbourne Old Town, turn left.*

3 *At the car park continue straight on following the yellow arrow.*

A Once clear of the sunken lane that leads up from the village, you can see across the valley to the hillside opposite, where low earth banks divide the land into a number of small fields. These are the so-called 'Celtic' fields, which were cultivated by Iron Age settlers before the Romans came to Britain.

B The 'ancient' stones at the top of the hill are, in fact, part of Eastbourne's old Barclays Bank! From the top of Babylon Down, there are superb views across Eastbourne to the sea, and back down the deep, shapely valley of Willingdon Bottom to Jevington.

C Jevington village is a charming spot of leafy lanes and pleasant, unostentatious houses. The church has a massive, square Saxon tower which is thought to have been used as a refuge at the time of the Viking raids. Inside there is a sculpture of the same period, showing Christ thrusting a sword into the mouth of the Beast.

Walk 2
CROWLINK AND THE SEVEN SISTERS
3 miles (4¾ km) Quite strenuous between points 3 and 4

0 ___ ¼ mile
0 ___ ¼ km

This route combines a pleasant stroll across typical, rough downland with an exhilarating walk over a section of the tall, chalk cliffs near Beachy Head, the Seven Sisters. Turn south off the A259 Seaford to Eastbourne road at Friston. The turning is between the church and the village pond, almost opposite the B2105 Jeving- ton road. The National Trust car park is approximately ¼ mile (400 m) up the road marked 'No Through Road'.

1 *From the car park, take the surfaced road that bends downhill to the right.*

8 *At the houses, turn left and return to the start.*

7 *Turn left through the bridle gate and head across the field to the gate opposite.*

Gayles

Friston

2 *At the end of Crowlink village, continue straight on along the bridleway.*

6 *Where the path divides, keep to the edge of the woods which drop away sharply to the right.*

P

Gap Bottom

Crowlink

National Trust

Seven Sisters (one of)

Went Hill

Birling Farm

Seven Sisters (one of)

(A)

Seven Sisters (one of)

Birling Gap Road

Seven Sisters (one of)

Birling Gap

3 *At the edge of the cliffs, turn left and follow the line of the cliffs.*

4 *At Birling Gap, head across the field towards the gate with a white house behind it.*

5 *Turn left up the broad track beside the houses and head straight up Went Hill towards a prominent red-roofed barn.*

A The chalk cliffs mark the southern end of the downland. The section of cliffs between Cuckmere Haven and Birling Gap rises and falls to present a wave-like profile. There are, in fact, eight crests but, presumably because it sounds rather more euphonious, they are always known as the Seven Sisters, and three of them are included on this walk. This is superb scenery with the cliffs rising more than 200 feet (60 m) above the sea. Most of the area is in the care of the National Trust. An obelisk marks a gift of land by W A Robertson, and a sarsen stone on a plinth records the handing over of the Crowlink valley by Viscount Gage of Firle. These generous gifts have ensured that this part of the coast will not be spoiled.

Walk 3

SEVEN SISTERS COUNTRY PARK 3 miles (4¾ km) Easy

This gentle walk down the valley of the Cuckmere to the sea is particularly recommended to bird-watchers, who can expect to see a rich variety of species, including such handsome visitors as the redshank and the shelduck. The walk is a clearly marked route through the Seven Sisters Country Park, established by East Sussex County Council in 1971. The car park is on the A259 Seaford to Eastbourne road at Exceat opposite Exceat Farm, 2 miles (3¼ km) east of Seaford.

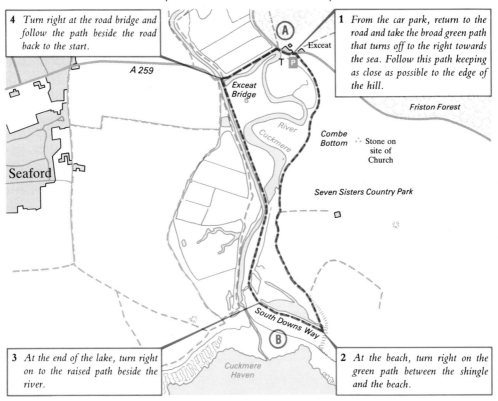

4 *Turn right at the road bridge and follow the path beside the road back to the start.*

1 *From the car park, return to the road and take the broad green path that turns off to the right towards the sea. Follow this path keeping as close as possible to the edge of the hill.*

3 *At the end of the lake, turn right on to the raised path beside the river.*

2 *At the beach, turn right on the green path between the shingle and the beach.*

A An eighteenth-century barn at Exceat Farm has been converted to provide a centre for the Seven Sisters Country Park, and additional barns house a natural history exhibition 'The Living World'. Exceat village is mentioned in Domesday Book as having three estates but it went into a decline and was united with West Dean in 1528.

B The Cuckmere River was canalized in 1846 to reduce flooding, and the path alternates between the meandering river and the straight lines of the canal. At Cuckmere Haven, a shallow lake with shingle islands have been formed to provide a feeding and nesting area for birds. At low tides you can see ironwork projecting from the sea near the mouth of the river. This is the wreck of the German ship, *Polynesia*, which sank in April 1890.

16

Walk 4
GLYNDE AND MOUNT CABURN 2½ miles (4 km) Moderate

0 ——————————————————————— 1 mile
0 ——————————————— 1 km

The walk begins in the village of Glynde, which lies to the north of the A27, 3 miles (5 km) east of Lewes. It is possible to park opposite the Post Office, close to the start of the walk.

As soon as one begins the slow, steady climb up through the fields, one becomes conscious of the great sense of spaciousness and the wide vistas which are the main features of this walk.

3 *Retrace your steps but continue past the original path from Glynde.*

4 *Two hundred yards (180 m) past the first Glynde turning, turn right on to the broad track by a farm gate.*

5 *At the roadway, turn right and return through the village to the start.*

Tumulus

Glynde Holt

Decoy Wood

Tumulus

Home Farm

Glynde Place

B

Ranscombe Camp

Glynde

A

Glynde Reach

Fort

Ranscombe Farm

Mount Caburn

A 27(T)

2 *At the top of the ridge, turn left for Mount Caburn.*

1 *Cross the stile opposite the post office and follow the path up the hill.*

A Mount Caburn is a prominent hill, occupying a strategic site, overlooking the confluence of the Ouse and the Glynde. The summit of the hill was a farmstead as long ago as 500 BC, but around 150 BC it was fortified by a great circular rampart and ditch that surround the whole hilltop area.

This Iron Age fortress was further strengthened by a wooden palisade, but all these efforts proved in vain, for the fort was attacked and overthrown by Roman legions.

The bank and ditch are still prominent features of the hill and, from the hill's summit, you can command magnificent views of all the surrounding countryside.

To the west, lies the town of Lewes, the county town of East Sussex. It was once an important inland port, guarded by its still prominent castle. When the barons of England, led by Simon de Montfort, opposed the dictatorial rule of Henry III, the issue was settled at the Battle of Lewes, and the subsequent treaty paved the way to parliamentary government. The woods and parkland to the north surround the mainly Tudor manor house of Glyndebourne. It was here in 1934 that John Christie established a music festival and then went on to build the opera house that is now world famous.

B Glynde Place is an attractive sixteenth-century house, much altered in the eighteenth century, and open to the public on certain days in the summer. It presents a handsome face to the road: the grand entrance through the stable block is flanked by a pair of ferocious wyverns – mythical winged dragons.

The nearby church comes as something of a surprise, a building of 1765 in the purely classical style that one might expect to find in a London street, but which looks curiously out of place in a Sussex village.

Walk 5
WILMINGTON AND LONG MAN
3¾ miles (6 km) Moderate

The village of Wilmington, with its many picturesque cottages, lies immediately south of the A27 between Polegate and Lewes. Drive through the village and the car park is just beyond the Priory. This is a walk that has something to appeal to everyone: it includes a typical section of undulating downland which, unlike the surrounding hills, is not cultivated but is covered by turf and furze. In contrast to this is the flat land of the valley through which the Cuckmere winds its way to the sea.

These two areas offer quite different habitats for wildlife, so that one moves from the high, tuneful call of the skylark rising above the hill to the croaking partridge, strutting unseen among the crops of the lower slopes, and on to find a variety of waterfowl down by the river.

But this is a walk which has its greatest appeal for those interested in history and the past, for it has a great variety of monuments, ranging from a Stone Age burial mound to a medieval priory and includes the enigmatic hillfigure, the Long Man.

A Wilmington Priory was built shortly after the Norman Conquest, for members of an Order from Grestain in France. It was probably used as an administrative centre for controlling the newly acquired estates in England. Part of the original building remains as a romantic ruin, but parts have also been restored and put to use as a small, agricultural museum which is open every day except Tuesday throughout the summer.

B The Long Man of Wilmington is a figure carved into the side of Wilmington Hill, showing the outline of a man, 200 feet (60 m) tall, arms outstretched, carrying two long spears or wands. He is certainly at least 1000 years old, but no-one can fix a precise date nor say what or who he is meant to represent. His stance is not unlike that of standard-carrying legionnaires shown on Roman coins but, equally, he also looks rather like a depiction of a Saxon stave-carrying warrior. He is, however, carved very accurately and is designed to be viewed from the valley, for, when seen from up the hill, the figure becomes foreshortened. No-one has the least idea as to why he was carved. But he is not the only feature of interest on the hill. As you look up at the Long Man, over to his left near the brow of the hill, you can see humps and hollows which mark the spot where Neolithic or New Stone Age man mined for flints, which he could then shape to make axes, arrowheads, or knives. And the long, low mound on the brow of the hill is a long barrow, where the Neolithic dead were buried.

C Burlough Castle is the name given to the promontory rising up above the river near Milton Street. There is a certain amount of controversy as to whether this is a natural or artificial feature. There certainly was a Norman castle of that name, but the original castle, a simple motte and bailey or mound and courtyard, might have been at the other set of earthworks, the Rookey, which can be seen a couple of hundred yards (180 m) to the north. Castle or not, this presents a splendid viewpoint from which to look up at the steep scarp slope of the Downs or out along the valley of the Cuckmere, dominated by the steeple of Alfriston church, while just across the river is old and stately Berwick Court.

Over

Walk 5
Wilmington and Long Man
continued

0   1 mile
|—————|—————|—————|—————|
0   1 km

8 *Where the paths cross, turn right straight down towards the road.*

9 *Turn left at the road.*

10 *Turn right on the grassy track beside the last house and return to Wilmington.*

7 *The road turns sharply to the right. Continue straight on along the sunken path.*

11 *Turn right at the road and return to the start.*

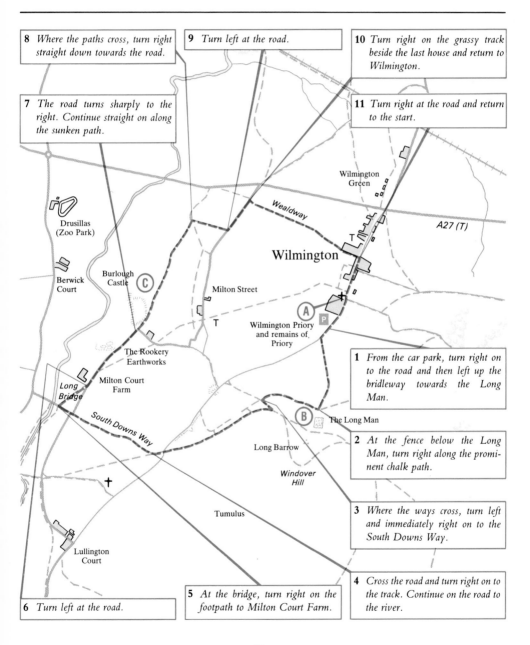

Wilmington Green

Drusillas (Zoo Park)

Wealdway

A27 (T)

Wilmington

Berwick Court

Burlough Castle (C)

Milton Street

Wilmington Priory and remains of Priory

The Rookery Earthworks

Long Bridge

Milton Court Farm

South Downs Way

(B) The Long Man

Long Barrow

Windover Hill

Tumulus

Lullington Court

1 *From the car park, turn right on to the road and then left up the bridleway towards the Long Man.*

2 *At the fence below the Long Man, turn right along the prominent chalk path.*

3 *Where the ways cross, turn left and immediately right on to the South Downs Way.*

4 *Cross the road and turn right on to the track. Continue on the road to the river.*

6 *Turn left at the road.*

5 *At the bridge, turn right on the footpath to Milton Court Farm.*

Walk 6

ALFRISTON AND BLACKSTONE BOTTOM

5½ miles (8¾ km) Moderate

The walk begins in the deservedly popular village of Alfriston, climbs to the top of the downland, and returns in a wide arc that takes in the lovely, sweeping and rolling countryside that stretches away behind the steep escarpment. Alfriston lies south of the A27 Eastbourne to Lewes road, and there are large public car parks at the north end of the village.

The first part of the walk takes you out through the hedges on the edge of Alfriston but, once clear of those, the steep climb, up the track of the South Downs Way, brings increasingly splendid views. To the south, sinuous valleys twist between rounded hills while, to the north, you look out over the broad expanses of the Weald. Where the track turns south again on to a green way, you have a superbly lonely tract of downland to enjoy. The final section of the walk, by way of contrast, brings you down through steep woods, then offers more downland and ends in a deep, shaded lane.

A From the top of Bostal Hill, there are superb views across the Weald to the distant hills of the North Downs. Up here, the cultivated ground has given way to rough grassland, pasture for grazing sheep. Immediately below is Alciston with its grand tithe barn, and, just to the west of it, is the curiously named Bopeep Farm.

B From the top of the ridge, one has the sensation of being at the very heart of typical downland countryside. The rise and fall of the ground produces a landscape full of soft shapes and sinuous curves, where the soft chalk has been gradually and slowly eaten away and weathered. To the north, the hill plunges down into a shapely amphitheatre; to the south it heaves and sways in a steady rhythm of ridge and valley before climbing steeply to the wooded escarpment that marks the edge of the Downs.

Birds provide a mixed chorus from the ever-present skylark, to the harsh rattle of the partridge from the cultivated fields, while the copses emit the hollow hooting cry of the woodpigeon, often joined in spring by the cuckoo, a very common summer visitor to the Downs.

C Alfriston is a village which well repays time spent on exploration. The route has been chosen to show some of its more interesting features. St Andrew's church stands at one side of the green known as the Tye. It is raised up on a grassy platform, which itself a site of ritual significance in prehistoric times. The present church was built in 1360 and is a superb example of how flint can be used to great decorative effect as a building material. The steeple is covered in wooden 'tiles' or shingles. It is a handsome building and it is easy to see how it has become known as 'The Cathedral of the Downs'.

Next to the church is a thatched, timber-framed house as old as the church itself. This is the Clergy House, built for the local priests; it was partly rebuilt in the seventeenth century following a fire: the timber work at the right-hand end of the façade can be seen to be different from that of the rest. It is historically important, for this was the very first house to be bought by the National Trust. The Vicar of Alfriston, the Reverend F W Benyon had been fighting for years to save the ancient building when he approached the newly founded Trust in 1894.

The houses in the main village street are not merely picturesque, but also display all the characteristic materials of the area: timber frames are filled with daub and plaster, or covered by weatherboarding or rich, red tiles. The most exotic building is the fifteenth-century Star Inn which, in its day, has been everything from a hostelry for pilgrims to a haunt of smugglers. The ferocious red lion outside was once the figurehead of a seventeenth-century Dutch warship.

Over

0   1 mile

0   1 km

5 *At the brow of the hill, go through the gate and turn left; and then immediately left again by the signpost with a blue arrow pointing to a path downhill through the woods.*

4 *At the top of the hill where the fields give way to rough grassland, turn sharp left on to the obvious track.*

3 *Where the path divides, take the right fork indicated by a blue arrow.*

2 *Continue up the hill on Kings Ride.*

1 *Leave the car park and go down the main village street. Turn right by the Star Inn on to the South Downs Way.*

Tumuli

(A)

South Downs Way

Cross Dyke

Tumulus

Green Way (Track)

Long Burgh
Long Barrow

Alfriston

(C)

Old Clergy House

River Cuckmere

Cross Dyke

(B)

9 *Turn right by the Wingrove Tavern to the church.*

8 *Turn left at the road.*

6 *At the edge of the woods, go through the bridlegate on the left and head through between the clumps of trees to the edge of the field as indicated by a blue arrow.*

7 *At the top of the hill, turn right by the fence.*

10 *Turn left down the narrow lane by the United Reformed Church and return to the main street.*

21

Walk 7

WEST FIRLE, FIRLE BEACON, AND BEDDINGHAM HILL

5 miles (8 km) Moderately easy; strenuous climb between points 3 and 4

The walk starts at West Firle which lies immediately south of the A27 Lewes to Eastbourne road, 4 miles (6½ km) from Lewes. There is limited parking space available in the village near the post office. As with many walks in this area that start in the valley bottom, one is immediately faced by a steep climb up the face of the scarp. Once at the top, however, where the South Downs Way is joined, reward for the effort arrives in the form of panoramic views. The landscape offers an intriguing mixture of the natural, the familiar pattern of fields and farms, and the formal parkland of the Firle Place estate.

A West Firle is dominated by the grand house, which is open to visitors on certain days during the summer. It is well worth while checking locally so that the walk can coincide with an open day. Firle Place has been the home of the Gage family since the fifteenth century but, although the present house has a Tudor core, what we now see is largely the result of a rebuilding in Georgian times.

The surrounding parkland is very much what one would expect from the eighteenth century, a carefully contrived landscape, dotted with trees and boasting an ornamental lake, in the style of Capability Brown.

The village church of St Peter emphasizes the importance of the Gage family to the village. The building itself has seen many changes, but mostly dates from the fourteenth and fifteenth centuries. Inside are some superb monumental brasses and tombs, particularly splendid is the Bolney Brass, showing Bartholomew Bolney dressed in armour with his wife, Eleanor, at his side. Of the three Gage tombs, the finest is that to Sir John Gage and his wife, Philippa, of 1556, the couple being beautifully sculpted in alabaster. The twentieth century, too, has brought a note of splendour to the church with a memorial window by the artist, John Piper, installed in 1985.

B Looking back from the steep path that runs up alongside Firle Planation, you can see a tall tower rising up among the trees to the south-east. This is no medieval fortification but a folly, designed both to enhance the view from Firle Place and to provide visitors with a panorama from its top.

C Beddingham Hill is dominated by the radio station with its tall mast. But there are other points of interest, even if they are not quite so conspicuous. To the east, the top of the escarpment is dotted with tumuli, round barrows used for burials. To the west, set among rough grass and gorse is White Lion Pond, a dew pond, probably constructed in the eighteenth century to provide water for grazing sheep. They are a feature of the Downs and, round them, as here, you can see a rich variety of wild flowers such as harebells and lady's bedstraw.

From here one can see across the Ouse valley, criss-crossed by the straight lines of drainage ditches, to the town of Lewes. To the south, the tall silhouettes of cranes mark where the river reaches the sea at Newhaven. You can also see how people have removed the chalk from the hillside by digging pits, the biggest of which marks the site of the Beddingham cement works closed in the 1970s.

The area immediately to the south, along which the route travels, shows a familiar pattern of farms strung out along the foot of the escarpment, taking advantages of the springs that flow out through the chalk.

Over

22

6 *At the end of the houses, turn right along the footpath marked to Firle.*

7 *At the road, turn right.*

8 *Take the road to the left, and return to the start.*

1 *Walk up the village street past the church and continue straight on along the footpath.*

2 *Where the way divides, follow the broad track round to the left.*

3 *At the avenue of trees, turn right up the edge of the wood and follow the path round to the top of the downs.*

5 *Two hundred yards (180 m) past the radio masts, where a gate crosses the South Downs Way, turn right and follow the path that sweeps round to the right. Head down the hill to Little Dene.*

4 *At the South Downs Way, turn right and walk on towards the prominent radio masts.*

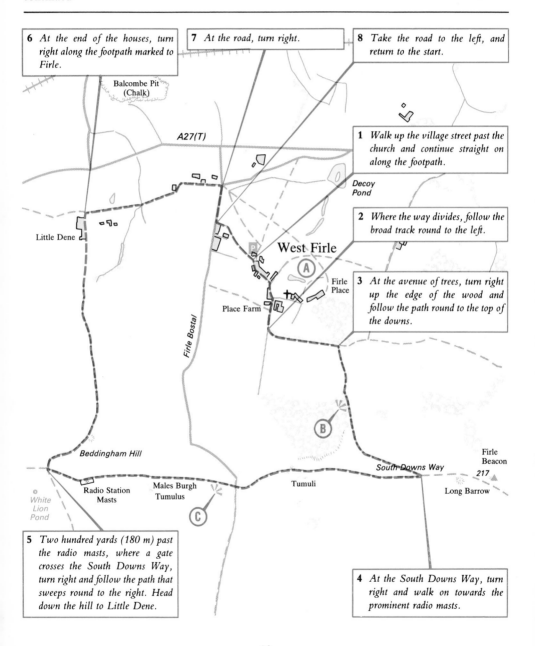

Balcombe Pit (Chalk)

A27(T)

Decoy Pond

Little Dene

West Firle

Firle Place

Place Farm

Firle Bostal

Beddingham Hill

White Lion Pond

Radio Station Masts

Males Burgh Tumulus

Tumuli

South Downs Way

Firle Beacon

217

Long Barrow

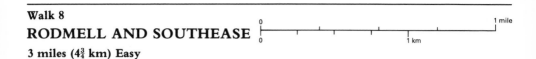

Walk 8
RODMELL AND SOUTHEASE
3 miles (4¾ km) Easy

To reach Rodmell, turn south at the roundabout on the A27 Brighton to Lewes road, along the road signposted to Kingston. Turn right at the T-junction and park in the village. This is a gentle walk in the flat river valley and along the banks of the tidal Ouse.

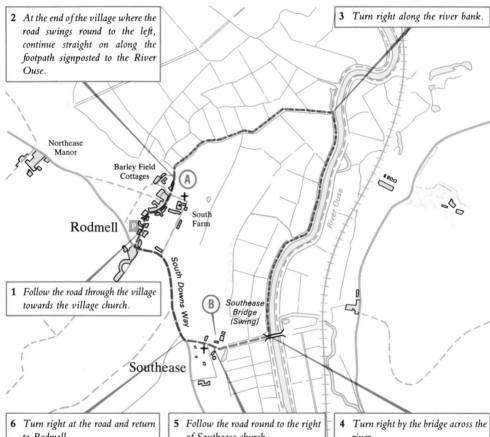

2 *At the end of the village where the road swings round to the left, continue straight on along the footpath signposted to the River Ouse.*

3 *Turn right along the river bank.*

1 *Follow the road through the village towards the village church.*

6 *Turn right at the road and return to Rodmell.*

5 *Follow the road round to the right of Southease church.*

4 *Turn right by the bridge across the river.*

A Rodmell is a quiet village, graced by a handsome Norman church. Nearby is the picturesque Monk's House, once the home of Leonard and Virginia Woolf and now owned by the National Trust.

B Southease is a delightful hamlet of traditional houses grouped round a green. Its main attraction is the church, with its unusual round tower. Inside are slightly faded wall paintings that date back to the thirteenth century.

Southease is now a quiet backwater, but was once a thriving fishing port: a reminder that large vessels had to use the river can be seen in the swing bridge over the river.

Walk 9
CISSBURY RING

1 mile

0   1 km

2 miles (3¾ km) Easy; steep climb at the beginning

Cissbury Ring is situated 1 mile (1½ km) south-east of Findon. The car park is signposted on the | A24 at Findon, ¼ mile (400 m) south of the dual carriageway. Turn into Maytree Avenue, then | Storrington Rise.

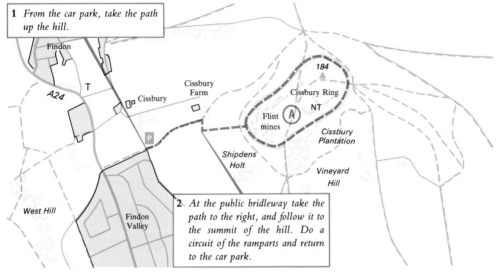

1 *From the car park, take the path up the hill.*

2 *At the public bridleway take the path to the right, and follow it to the summit of the hill. Do a circuit of the ramparts and return to the car park.*

A Cissbury Ring can immediately be recognized as an Iron Age hill fort, for the entire top of the hill, an area of 62 acres (25 ha), is surrounded by a high bank and deep ditch, with entrances to the south and the east. Hill forts, such as Cissbury, can be thought of as the major centres for the different Celtic tribes that populated Iron Age Britain. Many were given new, stronger defences at the time of the Roman invasion, but not Cissbury. The local tribe, the Atrebates were friendly to Rome and continued peacefully on their way. Indeed, the only marks that have survived from this period are the marks of the plough at the top of the plateau.

But people were busy here as long ago as 3000 BC. The deep depressions, surrounded by dough-nut-shaped mounds of earth, that scar the hillside, are the remains of Neolithic flint mines. In the New Stone Age, people began to app-reciate that some flints were better for their purposes than others – they were more easily knapped and shaped, they took a finer cutting edge, or a better polish.

These superior flints often lay in thick bands some way beneath the surface. So shafts were dug down to the flint, and the miners then travelled out from the base, using simple tools, such as the shoulderblade of an ox as a shovel and an antler as a pickaxe. There

was a limit to how far they could tunnel in this way, and when that limit was reached, they abandoned that mine and went on to sink another shaft. In time, the disused mines caved in leaving the charac-teristic hollows surrounded by their circular rings of spoil from the workings.

The walk around the rim of the hill not only provides ample opportunity to see the impressive fortifications, but also supplies constantly changing views. To the south is the popular holiday coast stretching from Worthing to the distant towers of Brighton; to the north lies the main ridge of the downs, dominated by the beeches of Chanctonbury Ring.

25

DITCHLING BEACON, LOWER STANDEAN, AND CLAYTON WINDMILLS 5½ miles (8¾ km) Moderate

The principal feature on this walk is Ditchling Beacon, one of the high points of the Downs just over 800 feet (245 m) above sea-level. There is a car park near the Beacon, but the suggested starting point is the car park at Clayton windmills, enabling the energetic to combine this walk with Walk 11 to Wolstonbury Hill.

The starting point is reached by turning east into Mill Road, which runs off the A273, ½ mile (800 m) south of the road junction with the B2112 at Clayton. The walk follows the South Downs Way for 2 miles (3¼ km), and then explores the rolling, undulating country to the south of the escarpment. Local names tell a good deal about the nature of the walk which goes past the long shallow valley of Hogtrough Bottom to the rough crest of Heathy Brow, from where one can look down on the regulated woodland of Highpark.

There is even a suggestion that golf is indeed a game for Everyman or Everywoman, as the Pyecombe course is laid out on the slopes of Middle Brow.

A There are two Clayton windmills, known as 'Jack and Jill', which is something of a break with tradition because sailing windmills are, like sailing ships, regarded as females. Jack, the larger of the two, was built in 1876 and is now privately owned. The second mill, Jill, is occasionally open to the public. This is the older of the two, built in 1821. It originally stood near Brighton but was moved to its present position around 1850.

They represent two different solutions to the problem facing all millers – how to keep the sails facing into the wind. Jill is a post mill, in which all the machinery is housed in the 'buck', the wooden housing to which the sails are attached. This whole structure is mounted on a central post, on which it can be pivoted. In its simplest form such a mill could be moved manually, but here there is a fantail mounted on the opposite side of the mill from the sails. When the sails face the wind, the fantail is becalmed but, if the wind shifts, it functions like a propeller to drive the mill round to the correct position.

Jack has a solid tower, and the sails and fantail are mounted on the top as a rotating cap.

B Ditchling Beacon itself is marked by a plinth, a triangulation point used by surveyors. Down below is the village of Ditchling which contains the fine old timbered building, Anne of Cleves' house. That lady did rather better than other wives of Henry VIII, for she kept her head, and the Ditchling estate, together with others in the area, came with the divorce settlement.

But the main attraction lies not in history, but in the majestic sweep of the Downs themselves for, in clear weather, the whole line of the Downs is laid out on view rolling back from its serpentine edge. Down below, the flat lands of the Weald appear speckled with dark-green patches, the remnants of the great forest that once covered the entire area. A more modern landmark can be seen between the beacon and the mills, the Keymer Post, a signpost that marks the boundary between recently created East and West Sussex.

Over

26

Walk 10
Ditchling Beacon, Lower Standean, and Clayton Windmills
continued

1 *From the car park, turn left on to the road up the hill, and continue straight on along the South Downs Way to Ditchling Beacon.*

2 *Retrace your steps for 200 yards (180 m) and turn left along the footpath marked to Heathy Brow.*

3 *Where bridleways cross, take the footpath to the right marked to Lower Standean and continue along the bottom of the valley.*

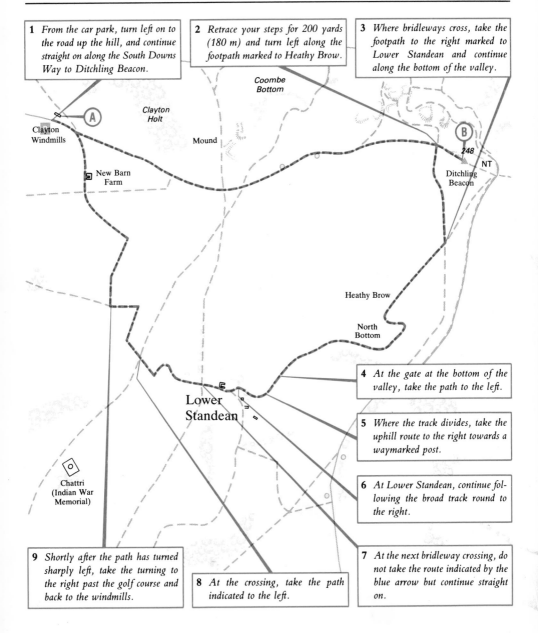

4 *At the gate at the bottom of the valley, take the path to the left.*

5 *Where the track divides, take the uphill route to the right towards a waymarked post.*

6 *At Lower Standean, continue following the broad track round to the right.*

9 *Shortly after the path has turned sharply left, take the turning to the right past the golf course and back to the windmills.*

8 *At the crossing, take the path indicated to the left.*

7 *At the next bridleway crossing, do not take the route indicated by the blue arrow but continue straight on.*

Walk 11

CLAYTON WINDMILLS AND WOLSTONBURY HILL

4 miles (6½ km) Moderately difficult; slightly strenuous between points 6 and 7

This walk, like Walk 10, begins at Clayton windmills. These are reached by turning east into Mill Road which runs off the A273, ½ mile (800 m) south of the road junction with the B2112 at Clayton. It can be combined with Walk 10 to make a long expedition, and a full description of the two windmills can be found in the notes to that walk. This is a pleasant walk with much of interest to see along the way, and culminating in one of those lofty Iron Age hill forts which are such a feature of the Downs. There is, however, a section of approximately 200 yards (180 m), where it is necessary to walk along the busy main road. In these circumstances, it is always advisable to walk on the right-hand side of the road, facing the oncoming traffic.

A Pyecombe is little more than a hamlet, but it boasts a fine church with excellent examples of Norman arches in the nave and an unusual decorated lead font, which is also Norman. The church also has a memento of the days when sheep rearing was the mainstay of the downland economy. The gate latch is made out of the curved iron top of a shepherd's crook, which was actually made in the building opposite. The single-storey extension to the house was once a forge specializing in the manufacture of crooks.

B The walk up Wolstonbury Hill is especially pleasant, a gentle track that curves round the edge of the bowl of Wellcombe Bottom, and gives fine views back across the valley to the two Clayton windmills that make an impressive appearance on the skyline. The ditches and ramparts at the summit mark it as an Iron Age fort, though they have been disturbed by flint digging.

Originally this was Wulfstan's burgh, which means Wulfstan's fortress and, from its commanding position giving views in every direction, it is obviously a very defensible situation. Today, the views are still there but now enjoyed simply for pleasure.

To the east in the valley below is Newtimber Place which looked to a moat for defence rather than an airy, hilltop site. To the west is the main London to Brighton railway line, which disappears from view – and the walk back takes you over the top of the Clayton tunnel. The tunnel was opened in 1841, and the northern entrance is marked by mock-medieval battlements. It was the scene of a tragic accident in 1861, when there was an underground collision between two trains in which twenty-three people were killed and 175 injured.

The way back down from the hill is a great contrast to the way up for, after a sharp descent of the hillside, the path plunges into woodland, as pleasant in its way as the open views of the grassy slopes.

Over

0   1 mile

0   1 km

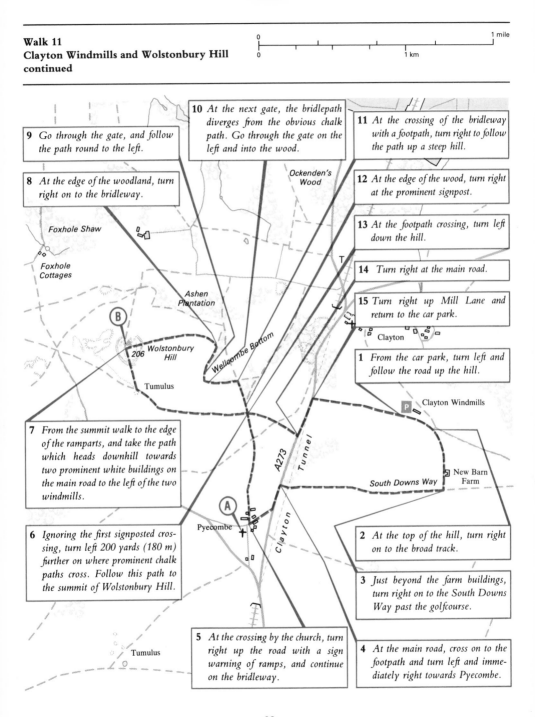

10 *At the next gate, the bridlepath diverges from the obvious chalk path. Go through the gate on the left and into the wood.*

9 *Go through the gate, and follow the path round to the left.*

8 *At the edge of the woodland, turn right on to the bridleway.*

11 *At the crossing of the bridleway with a footpath, turn right to follow the path up a steep hill.*

12 *At the edge of the wood, turn right at the prominent signpost.*

13 *At the footpath crossing, turn left down the hill.*

14 *Turn right at the main road.*

15 *Turn right up Mill Lane and return to the car park.*

1 *From the car park, turn left and follow the road up the hill.*

7 *From the summit walk to the edge of the ramparts, and take the path which heads downhill towards two prominent white buildings on the main road to the left of the two windmills.*

6 *Ignoring the first signposted crossing, turn left 200 yards (180 m) further on where prominent chalk paths cross. Follow this path to the summit of Wolstonbury Hill.*

2 *At the top of the hill, turn right on to the broad track.*

3 *Just beyond the farm buildings, turn right on to the South Downs Way past the golfcourse.*

5 *At the crossing by the church, turn right up the road with a sign warning of ramps, and continue on the bridleway.*

4 *At the main road, cross on to the footpath and turn left and immediately right towards Pyecombe.*

Foxhole Shaw

Foxhole Cottages

Ashen Plantation

Ockenden's Wood

(B)

206 Wolstonbury Hill

Welloombe Bottom

Tumulus

Clayton

Clayton Windmills

A273

Tunnel

South Downs Way

New Barn Farm

(A)

Pyecombe

Clayton

Tumulus

29

Walk 12

DEVIL'S DYKE, FULKING, AND POYNINGS

4½ miles (7¼ km) Moderately difficult; strenuous at the end

The Devil's Dyke car park is at the top of the Downs, immediately south of Poynings village. Drivers approaching from the north should turn south off the A281 on the minor road to Saddlescombe and Hove, 1 mile (1½ km) west of the junction with the A23. Take the first right turn beyond Saddles-combe and, after 1 mile (1½ km) turn right at the T-junction for Devil's Dyke.

Drivers arriving from the south should take the minor road to the north which leaves the A2038, 1 mile (1½ km) from the junction with the A23. Where the road forks, keep to the left and follow the road round to the car park at the top of the Dyke. For a short walk this offers a quite astonishing variety: there is some of the best and most spectacular downland scenery, a pleasant stroll across meadows watered by a meandering stream and two delightful villages.

A The Devil's Dyke itself is, in fact, a natural phenomenon, a deep valley with precipitous sides, biting deep into the Downs. The promontory formed between the Dyke and the escarpment made it an obvious choice for an Iron Age hill fort, and the ramparts, of earth bank and ditch, can be seen stretching across the neck of the promontory near the car park.

It has been a popular tourist attraction for 200 years, and the first hotel was built here in 1817. In 1879, the landlord decided to boost its popularity by building a mountain railway up the side of the Downs, the track of which can still be seen as a dark streak on the hillside when viewed from the valley near Poynings. He also built a cable-car ride across the gorge which must have been great fun.

B The Downs above Fulking give some idea of what most of the area was like until quite recently. Everywhere there is soft, springy turf where sheep and cattle graze instead of the fields of crops introduced by modern, mechanized farming. It adds immensely to the pleasure of walking.

Here you get superb views of the Downs escarpment, as it rises up from the valley floor, and it is easy to see how the villages keep close to the foot of the hills to take advantage of the springs emerging from the chalk. This is a favourite spot for hang-gliding.

C Just before reaching the village of Fulking, look out for a rather charming curiosity. The stile at the end of the steep path down through the woods has a special section that can be lifted to let dogs go through. The path emerges by the charming and popular pub, the Shepherd and Dog, where a spring burbles perpetually out through an ornate ceramic frame. Once, thousands of sheep were brought here to be washed every year. The walk takes you along the main village street, which meanders up the hill past a colourful array of thatched cottages.

D Poynings is named after the Poynings family who held the local manor for three centuries in the Middle Ages. The village is quite small, but the importance of the local family is reflected in the fine, cruciform church not unlike that at Alfriston, though it has no steeple on its sturdy, square tower. From here, one has a rather dauntingly clear view of the steep slope rising up to the top of the Devil's Dyke, a view which encourages many walkers to gather strength for the climb at the Royal Oak pub near the church.

Over

0 _____ 1 mile
0 _____ 1 km

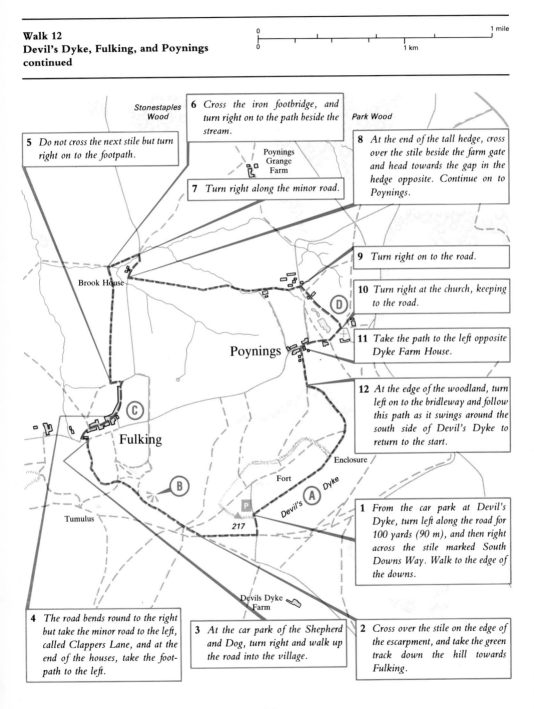

Stonestaples Wood

6 *Cross the iron footbridge, and turn right on to the path beside the stream.*

Park Wood

5 *Do not cross the next stile but turn right on to the footpath.*

Poynings Grange Farm

8 *At the end of the tall hedge, cross over the stile beside the farm gate and head towards the gap in the hedge opposite. Continue on to Poynings.*

7 *Turn right along the minor road.*

Brook House

9 *Turn right on to the road.*

10 *Turn right at the church, keeping to the road.*

Poynings

11 *Take the path to the left opposite Dyke Farm House.*

Fulking

12 *At the edge of the woodland, turn left on to the bridleway and follow this path as it swings around the south side of Devil's Dyke to return to the start.*

Enclosure

Fort

Devil's Dyke

Tumulus

217

1 *From the car park at Devil's Dyke, turn left along the road for 100 yards (90 m), and then right across the stile marked South Downs Way. Walk to the edge of the downs.*

Devils Dyke Farm

4 *The road bends round to the right but take the minor road to the left, called Clappers Lane, and at the end of the houses, take the footpath to the left.*

3 *At the car park of the Shepherd and Dog, turn right and walk up the road into the village.*

2 *Cross over the stile on the edge of the escarpment, and take the green track down the hill towards Fulking.*

Walk 13

CHANCTONBURY RING
AND WASHINGTON 4½ miles (7¼ km) Difficult

0 ————————————————————— 1 mile
0 ——————————— 1 km

Turn south off the A283, Steyning to Storrington road, about 2½ miles (4 km) west of Steyning on to a narrow, unclassified road signposted to Chanctonbury. The car park and picnic area are at the foot of the Downs.

5 *At the road, turn right and then immediately right again on the footpath just before the Frankland Arms.*

6 *At the edge of the wood, continue in the same direction through the woodland.*

7 *Turn left at the road and return to the start.*

1 *Turn left out of the picnic area and follow the path heading towards the hill; then climb up the hill on the public bridleway.*

Newcommon Copse

Tilleys Farm

Locks Farm

Washington

Quarry (dis)

Combe Holt

238 ▲

Cross Dyke

C

Chanctonbury Ring

Fort

Great Barn Farm

Tumulus

South Downs Way

Tumuli

Chalkpit Wood

A24

Cross Dyke

A

B

4 *At the point where a second South Downs Way sign appears, turn right on to the public footpath.*

3 *Follow the path to the right indicated as South Downs Way. It goes steeply downhill through a little wood.*

2 *At the top of the ridge, turn right on to the South Downs Way.*

A The walk up to the summit of the Downs is through mixed woodland, with views down towards Wiston House, home of Charles Goring who planted the Chanctonbury beeches.

B At the top of the Downs, the walk joins the South Downs Way in an area of open grassland. There are fine views over the Weald to the north and past the prominent, isolated Cissbury Hill to Worthing and the sea.

C Chanctonbury ring is a prehistoric earthwork, but it is now chiefly remarkable for its crown of tall beeches, that makes it the most prominent landmark on the Downs. Charles Goring brought the seedlings here when he was a boy in the 1760s, nurtured them, and lived to see them grow to maturity.

Walk 14
RACKHAM BANKS
5 miles (8 km) Moderate

```
0                                                          1 mile
|------|------|------|------|------|------|------|------|------|
0                                              1 km
```

Parking is to be found by Amberley Station, close to the point where the B2139 crosses the River Arun on Houghton bridge. This is approximately 1 mile (1½ km) from Amberley village, but this walk can easily be combined with Walk 16, for a contrasting day featuring both downland and watermeadows. This particular walk is very much a downland path, covering part of the South Downs Way itself and then exploring the rich, undulating country to the south of the ridge.

2 *Turn right at the road marked High Titton.*

3 *At the road junction, turn right and continue on the South Downs Way to Rackham Banks.*

4 *At the earthworks with prominent bank and ditch, turn right, leaving the little wood on your right.*

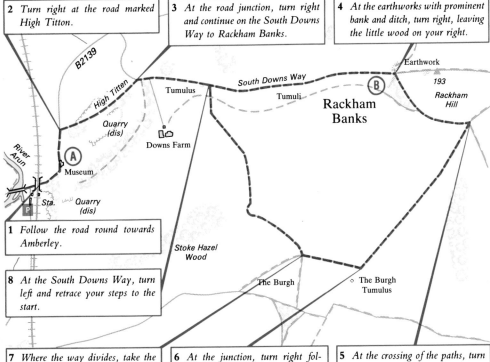

1 *Follow the road round towards Amberley.*

8 *At the South Downs Way, turn left and retrace your steps to the start.*

7 *Where the way divides, take the path to the right down into the deep valley and up again.*

6 *At the junction, turn right following the signpost with the yellow spot.*

5 *At the crossing of the paths, turn right as indicated by a signpost with a yellow spot.*

A The path climbs up the hill on a narrow ridge between two huge chalkpits. The pit to the south is now home to the Amberley Chalk Pits Museum, which is designed to show the working life of this part of England. It is currently open from Wednesday to Sunday through the summer, but walkers can get tantalizing glimpses of the exhibits through the screen of trees, including some of its impressive collection of narrow-gauge locomotives.

B Rackham Hill, the high point of this walk, commands extensive views over the Arun valley. Here, the path is crossed by the Rackham Banks, impressive prehistoric earthworks, the purpose of which is now unknown.

33

Walk 15

HIGHDOWN HILL AND CLAPHAM VILLAGE

0 _____ ½ mile
0 _____ ½ km

4½ miles (7¼ km) Moderately difficult; very muddy in wet weather

To reach Highdown Hill, turn north off the A259, Worthing to Littlehampton road, ¼ mile (400 m) west of the roundabout to the north of Goring, along a minor road, signposted to Highdown House. The car park is near the the top of the hill. The walk offers a mixture of downland, woods, and fields but does involve two crossings of the busy A27 trunk road.

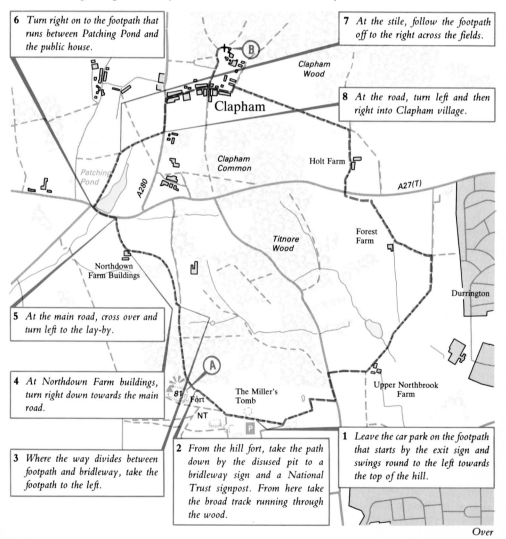

6 Turn right on to the footpath that runs between Patching Pond and the public house.

7 At the stile, follow the footpath off to the right across the fields.

Clapham Wood

Clapham

8 At the road, turn left and then right into Clapham village.

Clapham Common

Holt Farm

Patching Pond

A280

A27(T)

Titnore Wood

Forest Farm

Northdown Farm Buildings

Durrington

5 At the main road, cross over and turn left to the lay-by.

A

Upper Northbrook Farm

4 At Northdown Farm buildings, turn right down towards the main road.

81 Fort

The Miller's Tomb

NT

P

3 Where the way divides between footpath and bridleway, take the footpath to the left.

2 From the hill fort, take the path down by the disused pit to a bridleway sign and a National Trust signpost. From here take the broad track running through the wood.

1 Leave the car park on the footpath that starts by the exit sign and swings round to the left towards the top of the hill.

Over

34

0 ——————————————————— 1 mile
1 km

9 *At the end of the village street, go through the farm gate, turn left, and cross over the stile to the footpath across the fields.*

10 *At the wide lane, turn right.*

11 *Cross the main road; turn left down the lane, and then right at the footpath sign.*

12 *The track reaches a cottage. Cross over the stile on the left and head across the field.*

13 *Turn right into the lane.*

14 *At the stile, turn right and head across the fields towards the two chimneys of Upper Northbrook Farm.*

15 *At the roundabout, turn right.*

16 *Turn left at the road.*

17 *At the far end of the nurseries, turn right up the gated road and follow the track back to the car park.*

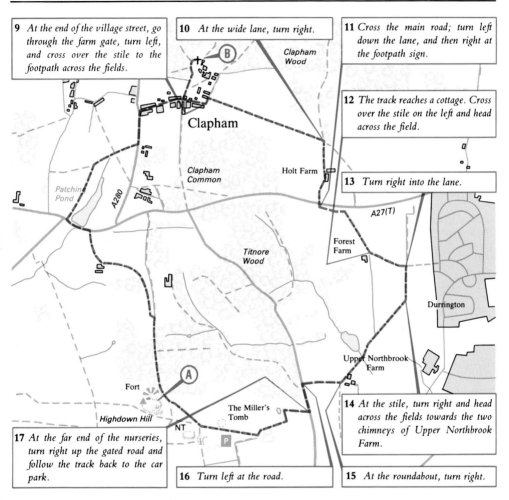

A Highdown Hill, like most isolated hills in Sussex, was fortified in the Iron Age. The ramparts and ditches are impressive, but they only enclose a small area. It is now a popular spot with visitors who enjoy the fine sea views, and, on a clear day, you can see as far as Beachy Head to the east and the Isle of Wight to the west.

B The village of Clapham seems mostly quite modern, until you realize that the old settlement was centred on the church a little further to the north among the woodland. The church itself dates mainly from the twelfth and thirteenth centuries, and contains sixteenth-century memorial brasses to the ancestors of the poet Shelley.

35

Walk 16

AMBERLEY WILD BROOKS

5 miles (8 km) Easy; boggy in parts

The walk begins in Amberley village, where there is street parking. This is quite unlike most of the other walks, and the name of the area covered – 'Amberley Wild Brooks' – gives a good idea of what to expect, even though it is, in fact, a corruption of 'Weald Brooks'. This is an area of water-meadows, swamp, and peat bog, rich with a varied flora, ranging from the bold colours of the yellow flag to the delicate bog rosemary. In summer it is busy with insects and waterfowl, including large flocks of geese. This walk can be combined with a contrasting downland excursion, Walk 14.

A Amberley village is one of the most attractive to be found along the whole Downs. The approach is dominated by the castle which occupies a site that has been fortified since before the Norman Conquest. The main fortifications date from the fourteenth century, when a great hall was built and a moat constructed. Over the years, it has been added to so that it has gradually changed from a dour, defensive stronghold to a comfortable family home, which it still is today.

The other focal point is St Michael's church, a very grand affair for such a small place, but reflecting the fact that the castle was home to the bishops of Selsey. It is predominantly Norman, and contains some slightly faded medieval wall paintings telling the story of the crucifixion. Amberley itself is a perfect example of a traditional Sussex village, with a wealth of attractive thatched houses and cottages.

B Rackham mill stands at the boundary between the rising, dry ground on which the hamlet stands and the watermeadows of the Wild Brooks. It was here that grain from the surrounding farms was brought to be ground into flour, the millstones being turned by an overshot waterwheel. This is a wheel in which the water arrives in a trough or 'launder', and then falls on to the top of the wheel, the force and weight of the water driving the wheel round.

From here, the walk goes on into an area of woodland – partly traditional downland species dominated by beech and oak, and partly modern coniferous plantation.

C Greatham bridge marked the old limit of navigation of the River Arun, and barges could still make their way this far up river right into the present century, while a few smaller craft could even reach as high as Pulborough.

The river here is tidal, with a rise of some 4 feet (1¼ metres) at spring tides, hence the need for protective flood banks.

D The final part of the walk is on a track across the bogs and marshes of the Wild Brooks. The straight lines of the drainage ditches show human attempts to tame and control this wasteland. It has been, at best, a partially successful attempt, and any straying from the track can lead to a walker disappearing over the ankles in thick, cloying ooze or peaty brown slime – so caution is very definitely needed. The rewards come, however, in walking an area which can convey a real sense of loneliness, with an atmosphere much closer to that of the fens of East Anglia than the chalk downland of south-east England. Trees line the drainage ditches and cattle graze on reclaimed land, but elsewhere the only inhabitants seem to be the birds and insects.

Over

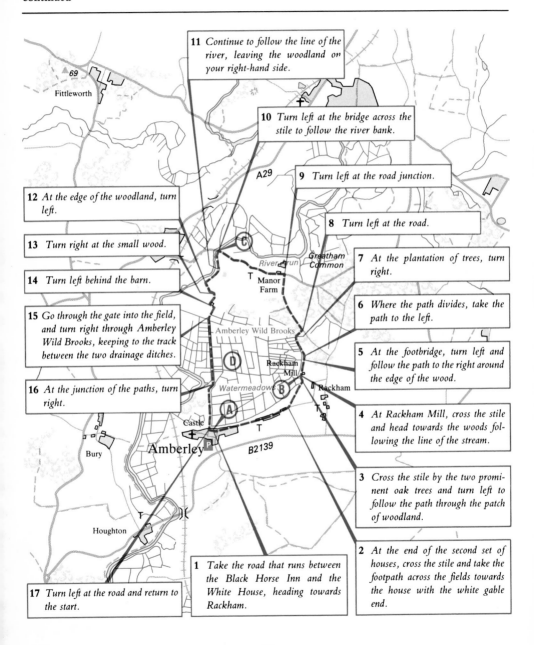

11 *Continue to follow the line of the river, leaving the woodland on your right-hand side.*

10 *Turn left at the bridge across the stile to follow the river bank.*

9 *Turn left at the road junction.*

8 *Turn left at the road.*

12 *At the edge of the woodland, turn left.*

13 *Turn right at the small wood.*

7 *At the plantation of trees, turn right.*

14 *Turn left behind the barn.*

6 *Where the path divides, take the path to the left.*

15 *Go through the gate into the field, and turn right through Amberley Wild Brooks, keeping to the track between the two drainage ditches.*

5 *At the footbridge, turn left and follow the path to the right around the edge of the wood.*

16 *At the junction of the paths, turn right.*

4 *At Rackham Mill, cross the stile and head towards the woods following the line of the stream.*

3 *Cross the stile by the two prominent oak trees and turn left to follow the path through the patch of woodland.*

2 *At the end of the second set of houses, cross the stile and take the footpath across the fields towards the house with the white gable end.*

1 *Take the road that runs between the Black Horse Inn and the White House, heading towards Rackham.*

17 *Turn left at the road and return to the start.*

37

Walk 17

ARUNDEL, BURPHAM, AND NORTH AND SOUTH STOKE

7 miles (11¼ km) Easy

The walk starts in Arundel at the car park by the bridge on the south bank of the river. In some ways, it is not unlike Walk 16, through the Amberley Wild Brooks but it offers an even greater variety of scenery. It is a walk which should prove particularly appealing to all those who enjoy studying bird and plant life, for it includes a section of totally un-tamed marshland and a walk past an extensive wildfowl reserve.

At the heart of the walk lies the River Arun which traces an extra-vagantly meandering path through its flood plain, on either side of which the hills rise steeply. Once the river was joined by canal to the Wey and then on to the Thames, forming a direct watery link between London and the south coast.

It takes something of an act of imagination now to think of this river being busy with trading barges, either under sail or being hauled along from the top of the high flood banks that protect the tidal river. A reminder of those days is to be found in the villages of North and South Stoke, one on each side of the river, which take their names from the stakes that once marked the channel at this point, where there was a ford in Roman times.

A At Burpham, the hills stick out a tongue towards the river in the form of a long promontory, which is climbed by a series of steps known as Jacob's Ladder. The promontory was once fortified, and guarded the river until the castle was built downstream at Arundel. Remains of the earth-works can still be seen above the steep, wooded slope that falls away to the river. The village of Burpham is a peaceful, beautiful spot, far enough off the beaten track to be largely ignored by the busy traffic of tourism. It boasts a fine, mainly Norman and Early English church, and a street of picturesque thatched cottages.

B Where the footpath leaves the high ground beyond Burpham to descend temporarily to the wet-land by the river, it runs along a low bank, behind which is an area of undrained swamp. This is a watery wilderness, seemingly as choked with lush vegetation and as impenetrable as any tributary of the Amazon. Reedbeds rise up among the trees, and a busy bird population can be heard but seldom seen among the thickets. It comes as quite a surprise to find such an untamed enclave in this corner of England.

C A triangle of wetland formed by the river, the wooded hillside, and a mill stream is now a wild-fowl reserve. The walk follows two sides of the triangle so there is ample opportunity to catch sight of some of the birds, whether they are home-grown species, such as the statuesque heron and the busy little coot, or more exotic residents preserved by the Trust, such as pintails and Bewick's swans.

D The town of Arundel is entirely dominated by the hugely impress-ive castle begun in 1067 by Roger de Montgomery. For the past 700 years, it has been the seat of the Dukes of Norfolk who have been the Premier Dukes of England since 1483. Like so many other fortresses, it was severely damaged in the Civil War, and was then not so much restored as largely rebuilt in the eighteenth and nineteenth centuries. The buildings seen today represent an idealized version of what a great castle should be, while inside is a sumptuous home rich in furnishings and works of art. The castle is regularly opened to the public during the summer. Down by the river are the ruins of the Maison Dieu, a hospice founded by the Fourth Earl of Arundel in 1396. Downstream is the old town quay, once lined with warehouses from the days when this was a busy port.

Over

38

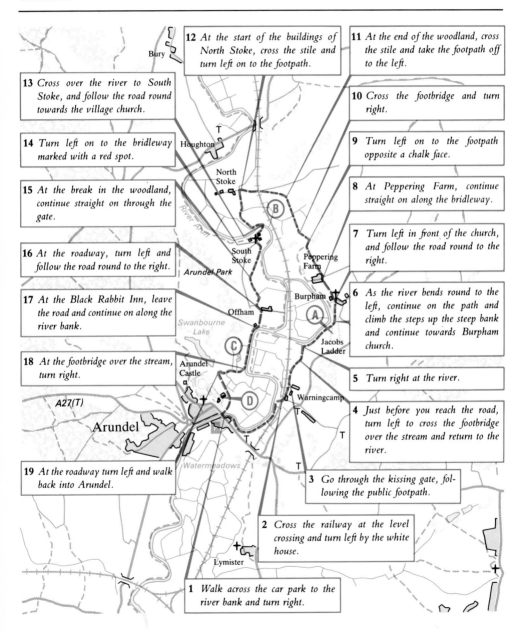

12 At the start of the buildings of North Stoke, cross the stile and turn left on to the footpath.

11 At the end of the woodland, cross the stile and take the footpath off to the left.

13 Cross over the river to South Stoke, and follow the road round towards the village church.

10 Cross the footbridge and turn right.

14 Turn left on to the bridleway marked with a red spot.

9 Turn left on to the footpath opposite a chalk face.

15 At the break in the woodland, continue straight on through the gate.

8 At Peppering Farm, continue straight on along the bridleway.

7 Turn left in front of the church, and follow the road round to the right.

16 At the roadway, turn left and follow the road round to the right.

6 As the river bends round to the left, continue on the path and climb the steps up the steep bank and continue towards Burpham church.

17 At the Black Rabbit Inn, leave the road and continue on along the river bank.

18 At the footbridge over the stream, turn right.

5 Turn right at the river.

4 Just before you reach the road, turn left to cross the footbridge over the stream and return to the river.

19 At the roadway turn left and walk back into Arundel.

3 Go through the kissing gate, following the public footpath.

2 Cross the railway at the level crossing and turn left by the white house.

1 Walk across the car park to the river bank and turn right.

Walk 18

BURTON MILL POND AND THE ROTHER VALLEY

3 miles (4¾ km) Easy

Burton Pond is a nature reserve managed jointly by West Sussex County Council and the Sussex Trust for Nature Conservation. The walk takes place mainly within the confines of the reserve, and incorporates the mill pond itself, the common and woodland on either side, and includes a brief look at the River Rother. To reach the start take the A285 south from Petworth and, after 2 miles (3¼ km) take a turn to the left, signposted Burton Mill. The mill itself is a mile (1½ km) down the road, and there is car parking at the mill.

A Burton Mill had long been disused, but was restored and put back to work in 1978, and it has also been opened to the public as a museum. It has an interesting history. The first and most obvious feature is the enormous mill pond which was originally constructed to provide water for a wheel that would work the massive hammers of an iron forge. The grain mill was built in 1781 with two water wheels, but these were replaced by water turbines earlier this century. It is one of these turbines that now drives the mill.

B The path passes through parkland, which was landscaped in the eighteenth century, and the sweet chestnuts which were planted at that time have now grown to massive proportions. Another landscape feature is the ornamental lake, Chingford Pond. The path crosses a causeway between this and the hammer pond, and it is interesting to compare the two. The ornamental lake has suitably picturesque, uneven boundaries, and there are the remains of a grotto and cascade by the path, while the latter is strictly functional. Both are home to a variety of waterbirds, which have made their home among the reeds, including grebe, mallard, coot, and moorhen.

C A causeway takes walkers safely through the peat bog in the middle of the woodland of Welch's Common. There is a number of rare water plants to be seen here, such as the delicate pink and white bogbean. The woodland of birch, oak, and alder is home to fallow and roe deer, but these shy creatures are rarely seen. Far more common and very visible are the wood ants that swarm over the pathways in the drier parts of the woodland.

D The walk encounters two disused transport systems. The first to be met is a cutting on what was a branch line of the London, Brighton, and South Coast Railway from Midhurst to Pulborough. The tracks have gone but the banks of the cutting make an ideal home for rabbits which can be seen scampering all over the old line. The next route is the River Rother, which was made navigable by artificial cuttings in the 1790s. It has long since become disused, and the canalized sections have dried up, leaving only the peaceful natural river.

Over

0   1 mile

0   1 km

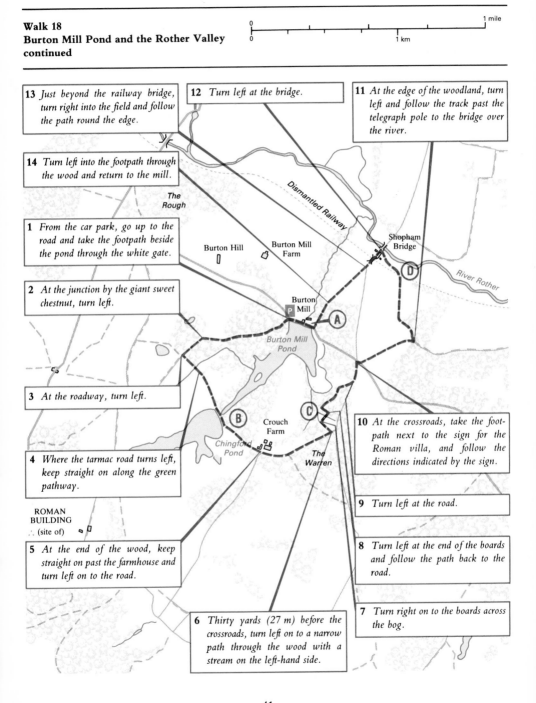

13 *Just beyond the railway bridge, turn right into the field and follow the path round the edge.*

12 *Turn left at the bridge.*

11 *At the edge of the woodland, turn left and follow the track past the telegraph pole to the bridge over the river.*

14 *Turn left into the footpath through the wood and return to the mill.*

The Rough

1 *From the car park, go up to the road and take the footpath beside the pond through the white gate.*

Burton Hill

Burton Mill Farm

Shopham Bridge

2 *At the junction by the giant sweet chestnut, turn left.*

Burton Mill

River Rother

P

(A)

Burton Mill Pond

(D)

3 *At the roadway, turn left.*

(B)

Crouch Farm

(C)

Chingford Pond

The Warren

10 *At the crossroads, take the footpath next to the sign for the Roman villa, and follow the directions indicated by the sign.*

4 *Where the tarmac road turns left, keep straight on along the green pathway.*

9 *Turn left at the road.*

ROMAN BUILDING
(site of)

5 *At the end of the wood, keep straight on past the farmhouse and turn left on to the road.*

8 *Turn left at the end of the boards and follow the path back to the road.*

7 *Turn right on to the boards across the bog.*

6 *Thirty yards (27 m) before the crossroads, turn left on to a narrow path through the wood with a stream on the left-hand side.*

Dismantled Railway

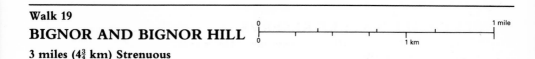

Walk 19
BIGNOR AND BIGNOR HILL
3 miles (4¾ km) Strenuous

Bignor lies on a minor road, between Duncton on the A285 and Bury on the A284. The road is signposted 'Bignor Roman Villa'. There is limited parking space available in the village. This is a walk through typical downland woods, with their preponderance of beech trees, and along the crest of the Downs.

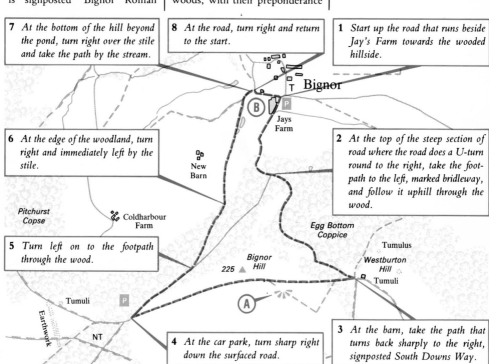

7 *At the bottom of the hill beyond the pond, turn right over the stile and take the path by the stream.*

8 *At the road, turn right and return to the start.*

1 *Start up the road that runs beside Jay's Farm towards the wooded hillside.*

Bignor

6 *At the edge of the woodland, turn right and immediately left by the stile.*

New Barn

2 *At the top of the steep section of road where the road does a U-turn round to the right, take the footpath to the left, marked bridleway, and follow it uphill through the wood.*

Pitchurst Copse

Coldharbour Farm

Egg Bottom Coppice

5 *Turn left on to the footpath through the wood.*

Tumulus

Bignor Hill

225

Westburton Hill

Tumuli

Tumuli

Earthwork

NT

4 *At the car park, turn sharp right down the surfaced road.*

3 *At the barn, take the path that turns back sharply to the right, signposted South Downs Way.*

A When the path eventually winds its way up to the top of the hill where it joins the South Downs Way, it emerges near a mounting block, the Toby Stone – a memorial to the fox-hunter, James Fitzwilliam-Toby and his wife Beryl. As always, there are extensive views from the summit but here, moving towards the western end, it is increasingly dominated by wide tracts of woodland. Bignor Hill was pre-sented to the National Trust in 1950. Just south of the walk, you can see a circle of rough grass, marked out by a low bank. This is a Neolithic causeway camp, probably a stock enclosure.

B Bignor itself is little more than a hamlet, though a delightful one. The church is essentially Norman, with an early Norman font, but the interior has suffered a good deal from the heavy hand of its Victorian restorer. Bignor's chief claim to fame is not actually on the walk, but those with time to spare will not be disappointed if they walk ½ mile (800 m) or so to the east and visit the Roman villa. It is famous for its beautiful mosaic pavements, of which the finest shows Zeus disguised as an eagle carrying away Ganymede.

Walk 20
KINGLEY VALE NATURE RESERVE
3¾ miles (6 km) Moderately difficult; strenuous at times and very muddy in wet weather

Kingley Vale is reached by taking a turning to the north off the B2178 at East Ashling, where the road makes a right-angled turn. At the T-junction, turn left and the car park is immediately on the right.

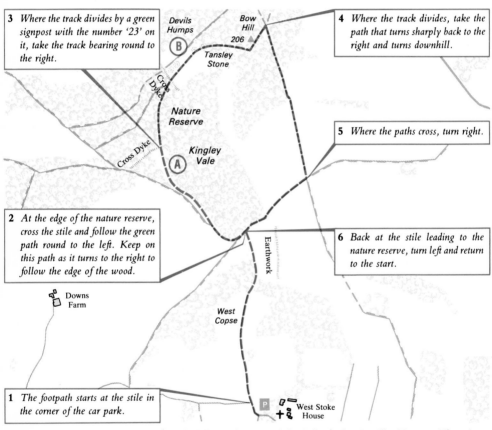

3 *Where the track divides by a green signpost with the number '23' on it, take the track bearing round to the right.*

4 *Where the track divides, take the path that turns sharply back to the right and turns downhill.*

5 *Where the paths cross, turn right.*

2 *At the edge of the nature reserve, cross the stile and follow the green path round to the left. Keep on this path as it turns to the right to follow the edge of the wood.*

6 *Back at the stile leading to the nature reserve, turn left and return to the start.*

1 *The footpath starts at the stile in the corner of the car park.*

Devils Humps
Bow Hill
206
Tansley Stone
Cross Dyke
Nature Reserve
Cross Dyke
Kingley Vale
A
B
Earthwork
Downs Farm
West Copse
West Stoke House

A The principal feature of the Kingley Vale Nature Reserve is the yew tree grove, which is said to be the finest of its kind in Europe. Some of the trees are as much as 500 years old. Much of the forest is quite dense, and the path follows the rim of the vale where the trees cling to the precipitous hillside.

B At the top of the hill is the superb row of Bronze Age burial mounds, or barrows, known as the Devil's Humps. The views from here are also very fine, looking out over the Downs to the north to Butser Hill and south to Chichester and the Isle of Wight.

EARTHAM WOOD AND STANE STREET

4½ miles (7¼ km) Moderate

The walk begins in the Forestry Commission car park in Eartham Wood. To reach the walk, take the minor road that turns east off the A285 Petworth to Chichester road, 4 miles (6½ km) south of Duncton. The car park can be seen on the left, approximately ½ mile (800 m) from the turning. Unlike many modern plantations, the woodland offers a mixture of deciduous trees and conifers, which greatly add to its interest. Although much of the walk lies through woods and copses, it is never dull, and is especially attractive in the early morning when the walker is likely to be alone with only the sound of birds to disturb the quiet. Where the walk does emerge into the open, it comes out to a gently rolling landscape of farmland spread over the lower slopes of the Downs.

A Six bridleways meet near the edge of Eartham Wood, but the route which this path follows clearly has a different character from the rest. It heads straight uphill without a sign of any deviation, all the way to the horizon, and appears as a broad track raised on a slight embankment above the level of the surrounding country.

It is, in fact, a Roman road, Stane Street, which ran from Londinium, or London, to Regnum, present-day Chichester. All this section of the road is well preserved and shows typical Roman engineering techniques. The surface was laid on top of an embankment, or agger which, in some sections on this walk, is as much as 50 feet (15 metres) wide and 4 feet (1.2 m) high. This provided good drainage which was improved by ditches cut at the sides of the road, which can still be seen. It would originally have been surfaced with broken flint and gravel. The line could be followed on quite easily, past the Roman villa at Bignor, and all the way on to finish at London Bridge. But even this short section impresses one with the skill of the military engineers of nearly 2000 years ago.

Over

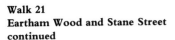

Walk 21
Eartham Wood and Stane Street
continued

0   1 mile

0   1 km

3 *Turn right along the bridleway that leads down across a field, past the barns of Gumber Farm.*

4 *Where the path divides by a pond, take the route to the left through the wood.*

5 *At the edge of the wood, take the green path to the right.*

2 *At the broad gravel path, marked as Stane street, turn left. The gravel path swings immediately to the left, but keep straight on along the stony green track.*

1 *Starting in the car park facing the road, take the path to the left.*

Gumber Farm

Stane Street

ROMAN ROAD

North Wood

Forestry Commission (A)

Eartham Wood

P

North Barn Farm

Eartham

T

8 *At the edge of the clearing where the prominent track swings left, carry straight on.*

9 *Turn right at the road and return to the car park.*

7 *At the next patch of woodland, take the path to the left.*

6 *Take the footpath to the right 30 yards (27 m) beyond the stile.*

45

Walk 22

SLINDON AND SLINDON WOODS

3 miles (4¾ km) Easy

The walk begins in the National Trust car park in Slindon Wood. Slindon is situated just north of the A27 between Chichester and Arundel. Turn off the A27 at Fontwell on to the A29. Almost immediately, you come to the imposing entrance to the Slindon Estate. Turn left on to the unclassified road signposted to Eartham and you will come to the car park after less than ½ mile (800 m) on the right. Slindon Wood is a part of a large estate and surrounds the extensive park. The National Trust owns over 3000 acres (1200 ha) of the estate, including a large part of Slindon village.

A The chief glory of Slindon Wood lies in its majestic beech trees and its fine oaks which set the dominant note for this part of the walk. The history of this park goes back a long way, and here you can see how the ancient woodland was marked out by a bank and ditch. This marked out the original park, which was not the sort of park we tend to think of today with flower beds and lawns, but an enclosed area of forest preserved for deer in medieval times. At the edge of the wood, if you look north, you can see a reminder of the eighteenth-century notion of parkland as countryside to be admired. On the hill is a mock ruin, a folly known as an eyecatcher, for it was literally intended to catch the eye of the stroller in the park.

B The most prominent building in Slindon village is the Park, begun in the thirteenth century, rebuilt in Tudor times, and considerably altered again over the years. It is now a school. The church, like many country churches, was a Norman foundation, greatly altered like the great house over the years and suffering the final indignities of Victorian restoration. It does, however, contain an unusual wooden effigy of a Tudor knight. The village itself has a number of attractive flint cottages and can boast two famous citizens, Hilaire Belloc and Richard Newland, one of the originators of cricket. It also has one charming curiosity: it is not uncommon to see an old railway carriage pressed into service as a summer house, but it is very rare to see a carriage with a thatched roof!

Over

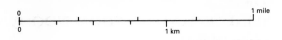

Walk 22
Slindon and Slindon Woods
continued

0 ———————————— 1 mile
0 ———————————— 1 km

4 *At the campsite, turn left, then right on to the road.*

5 *In the village, turn right along Church Hill.*

6 *Turn right at the T-junction.*

7 *At the next road junction, continue straight ahead on the footpath beside Park Lane.*

3 *Turn left at the junction of the paths.*

2 *Where the track divides, take the right-hand fork.*

Madehurst Wood

Park Pale

Ⓐ

✝

Slindon

Slindon Quarry (disused)

Ⓑ

A29

1 *From the car park, go through the gate and turn left on to the track through the woods.*

T

NT

Ⓟ

Slindon Wood

NT

Slindon Common

NT

8 *Just before the road, turn right on to the footpath through the woods.*

Fontwell Park Race Course

Fontwell

A27(T)

9 *Turn right at the road, and then immediately left on to the track by the National Trust sign.*

Walberton

12 *Leave the wood by the gatehouse and take the road to the right, signposted to Eartham, and return to the start.*

11 *Where the paths divide, keep straight on.*

10 *Where the path divides, take the path to the right.*

Walk 23
COCKING AND HEYSHOTT DOWN
3¾ miles (6 km) Strenuous

The walk begins at Cocking village on the A286, and there is parking space available in the village. The two villages of Cocking and Heyshott, met along the walk, have very different characters, as do the different sections of the walk itself.

The first part is a gentle stroll through farmland at the foot of the Downs. This is followed by a steep climb up through woodlands to join the South Downs Way, which is then followed along the crest of the hill, until another steep path takes you down again and back to the start.

A Heyshott is one of those villages which seem scarcely touched by the modern world. It is tucked away in a sheltered hollow, hemmed in by the woodland of the Weald and the steeply rising slopes of the Downs. It lies on a no through road so only those who want to come to Heyshott arrive here. Once it had its moated manor, but now it is a cluster of farms, cottages, a village green, and a memorial inside records its most famous parishioner, Richard Cobden, leader of the Anti Corn Law League.

It seems odd to think that the man who fought so hard against the agricultural interest of Victorian England should himself have lived in such a remote, rural village. The church can also boast three fine, antique bells, the oldest having been cast at the end of the fourteenth century. The walk into the village takes you past a cottage with a massive yew hedge.

B The approach to Heyshott Down is along a sunken lane, the high banks topped by hedges, rich with hedgerow plants, and busy with insects, with a rich variety of butterflies to be seen in early summer. The mixed woodland, predominantly beech and oak, that covers the hillside is coloured and the air is sweetened by clumps of wild rose and honeysuckle. At the top of the Downs, the open hillside is also made colourful by patches of heather, a plant rarely found on the chalk. It was this, in fact, which gave Heyshott its name, which literally means 'Corner in the Heather'. Charlton Forest which blankets the countryside to the south is home to deer, which can often be seen grazing at the edge of the trees, though they scamper off for cover very rapidly when humans appear.

C The descent into Cocking goes steeply downhill past a still-worked chalkpit to emerge by the clear, bubbling water of a spring. Beside it stands the village church, which is really quite grand. It is well worth exploring, if only to see the thirteenth-century wall painting of the angel appearing to the shepherds at the Nativity. The anonymous painter clearly took the men of the downs as his model; they are shown with their sheepdog, and one of the shepherds carries an old-style Sussex crook.

Beyond the church is the old village mill pond and mill cottage. The centre of the village now has a busy main road running through, but also has its memory of the famous local inhabitant in the friendly Richard Cobden pub.

Over

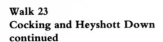

Walk 23
Cocking and Heyshott Down
continued

0   1 mile

0   1 km

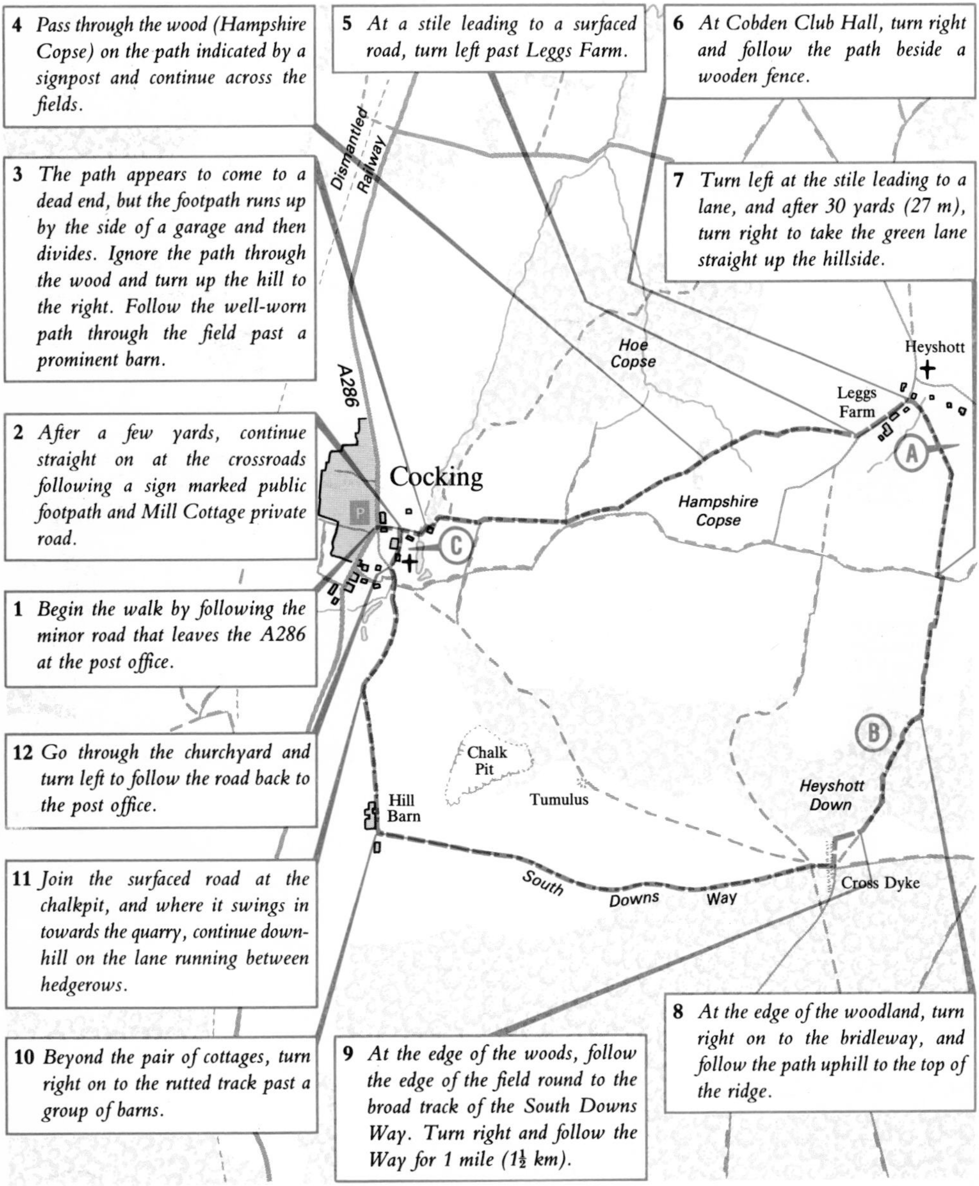

4 *Pass through the wood (Hampshire Copse) on the path indicated by a signpost and continue across the fields.*

5 *At a stile leading to a surfaced road, turn left past Leggs Farm.*

6 *At Cobden Club Hall, turn right and follow the path beside a wooden fence.*

3 *The path appears to come to a dead end, but the footpath runs up by the side of a garage and then divides. Ignore the path through the wood and turn up the hill to the right. Follow the well-worn path through the field past a prominent barn.*

7 *Turn left at the stile leading to a lane, and after 30 yards (27 m), turn right to take the green lane straight up the hillside.*

2 *After a few yards, continue straight on at the crossroads following a sign marked public footpath and Mill Cottage private road.*

1 *Begin the walk by following the minor road that leaves the A286 at the post office.*

12 *Go through the churchyard and turn left to follow the road back to the post office.*

11 *Join the surfaced road at the chalkpit, and where it swings in towards the quarry, continue downhill on the lane running between hedgerows.*

10 *Beyond the pair of cottages, turn right on to the rutted track past a group of barns.*

9 *At the edge of the woods, follow the edge of the field round to the broad track of the South Downs Way. Turn right and follow the Way for 1 mile (1½ km).*

8 *At the edge of the woodland, turn right on to the bridleway, and follow the path uphill to the top of the ridge.*

Map labels: Dismantled Railway, A286, Hoe Copse, Heyshott, Leggs Farm, Cocking, Hampshire Copse, A, C, P, B, Chalk Pit, Hill Barn, Tumulus, Heyshott Down, South Downs Way, Cross Dyke

HARTING DOWNS AND BEACON HILL

3½ miles (5½ km) Difficult; strenuous in parts

```
0                    ½ mile
├────┼────┼────┼────┤
0                 ½ km
```

The walk begins at the Harting Down car park on the B2141, approximately a mile (1½ km) south of South Harting. It incor- porates some of the best of the scenery of the South Downs, including the highest point of the Downs, nearly 800 feet (242 m) above sea-level, with wide views over the surrounding countryside. It also includes sections of fine, mixed woodland.

1 *Walk to the edge of the downs to the signpost indicating South Downs Way, and turn right.*

2 *Where the way divides, continue straight on to the top of Beacon Hill.*

3 *At the foot of the hill, turn right on to the South Downs Way as it bends sharply back.*

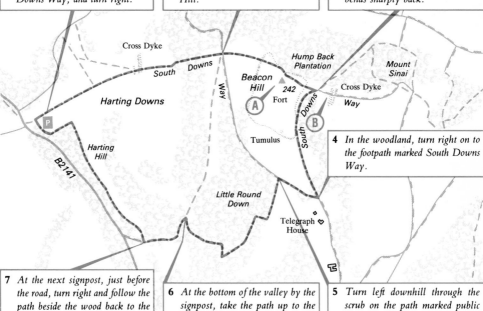

4 *In the woodland, turn right on to the footpath marked South Downs Way.*

7 *At the next signpost, just before the road, turn right and follow the path beside the wood back to the start.*

6 *At the bottom of the valley by the signpost, take the path up to the left through the woods.*

5 *Turn left downhill through the scrub on the path marked public footpath.*

A The high point is reached at Beacon Hill, which stands on a solitary plateau providing a com- plete view through 360 degrees: from the Weald to the north to the sea in the south; from the long expanse of the Downs stretching back to Chanctonbury Ring to the east, to the end of the ridge near Winchester to the west. The plateau of Beacon Hill was, inevi- tably, adapted as a hill fort in the Iron Age, though there are no very pronounced earthworks – the steepness of the ascent provid- ing, as walkers soon discover, quite adequate protection. The view from the top shows how the countryside through which the walk passes alternates between deep valleys, the sides spotted with scrub and gorse, and typical Downs woodland of beech and oak. Those who find the climb a little too steep, can take the path round the base of the hill to the south.

B The valley between Beacon Hill and Pen Hill to the east was fortified by cross dykes, which can still be seen as a pattern of bank and ditch cutting across the line of the South Downs Way.

Walk 25
QUEEN ELIZABETH COUNTRY PARK

0   ½ mile
0   ½ km

2 miles (3½ km) Easy

This walk is an adaptation of some of the waymarked routes within the Queen Elizabeth Country Park, designed to combine the most interesting elements of the many different walks laid out there.

The park itself lies to the east of the A3 Petersfield to Havant road. Access is via a signposted slip road 4 miles (6 km) south of Petersfield. There is a charge for use of the car park.

The greater part of the walk is through the forest and, although the park is close to a busy main road, the wood is so dense that there is a sense of complete peace and remoteness.

There is a great deal of variety within the woodland, which combines native trees, such as oak, whitebeam, and silver birch, with imports such as the now-familiar forest tree, the Corsican pine and the attractive southern beech. The park authorities have added to the interest with special features, such as the pond constructed in 1975.

2 *Return to the car park and follow the path round through the wood and past the park centre to the route marked with a yellow arrow as Holt Trail (yellow arrows will be seen at every turning point).*

1 *Take the path beside the main entrance to the car park and follow it round under the main road to the Butser Ancient Farm.*

8 *Continue across the broad path and take the path downhill to the left back to the centre.*

Newbarn Road

Ⓐ

Ⓟ

Queen Elizabeth Forest

3 *Cross the road and continue straight on.*

4 *Where the paths divide, turn left.*

Roman Building (site of)

7 *Turn left on to the broad path and then immediately right.*

5 *At the broad green path, continue straight on.*

6 *Turn right at the yellow post.*

A3(T)

A Butser Hill provides a total contrast to the dense and often dark woodland. It is an area of open grassland, rising almost 1000 feet (300 m) above sea-level.

The great attraction here, however, lies not so much in the scenery as in the Butser ancient farm. Archeologists set out to recreate an Iron Age farm, which would not just be a group of buildings using the materials and designs of some 2500 years ago, but would also use agricultural techniques of that period.

So here one can see Iron Age crops in the fields and farm animals that would have been bred and raised at that period. Crafts and skills of the period are also demon-strated. The principal feature is a round house, based on excavations made on an Iron Age site in Dorset.

The walk goes round the outside of the farm project, but there is a charge made for those who want to go inside for a closer look.

Walk 26

BURITON VILLAGE AND OLD DITCHAM

3¾ miles (6 km) Moderate; muddy when wet

Buriton is an attractive village reached by a minor road that turns east off the A3, slightly more than a mile (1½ km) south of Petersfield. There is adequate parking in the village, particularly in the area where the walk starts by the village pond and the church.

This route comes right up to the edge of the county boundary between Hampshire and West Sussex, which marks the end of the official South Downs Way. As one might expect from a walk at the end of the official long-distance path, it does not boast the drama of wide vistas that are such a mark of the routes that touch the top of the chalk ridge, but instead offers the quieter pleasure of shady country lanes, woodland, and pasture. This is a walk through a very English countryside.

A The village of Buriton is quite large, but is still dominated by the twin pillars of village life, church and manor house. The latter is a fine establishment, looking out over pasture, where grazing sheep dot the green. It is chiefly remembered today as the former home of the famous historian, Edward Gibbon. The church is unusually grand for a village, but once served a wide area, including the parish of Petersfield. It is handsome, if unpretentious, and has a set of Ringers' Rules in the bell tower which begins

Advice to ringers and to such
That delight in bells and love
  ye Church
Beware of oaths and
  quarrelings
Take heed of clams and
  janglings
There is no musik played or
  sung
Like unto bells if they are
  well rung

The scene created by manor, church, and shady village pond is one of the most delightful to be met on the whole South Downs.

B The descent back down to Buriton through the woods is on a path known as the 'Milky Way'. This is an old, hollow way, once regularly used by both pack animals and waggons, cut deep into the hillside by generations of users. The name probably originates in the profusion of white flowers of ramsons that line the route.

Over

0   1 mile
0   1 km

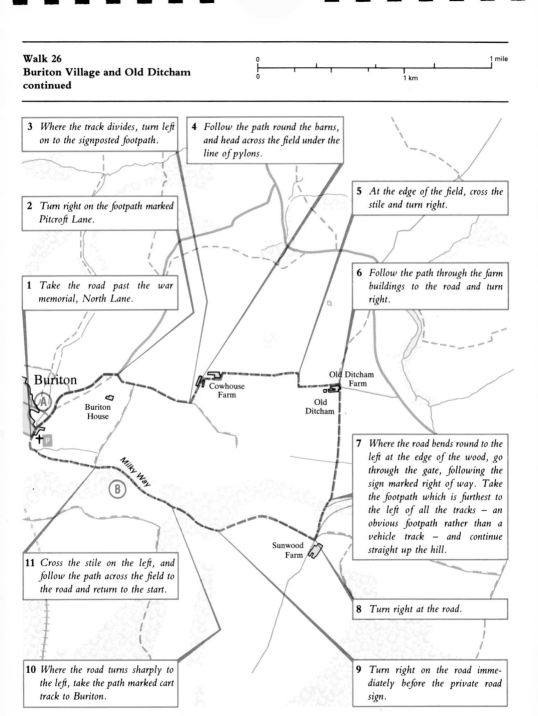

3 *Where the track divides, turn left on to the signposted footpath.*

4 *Follow the path round the barns, and head across the field under the line of pylons.*

5 *At the edge of the field, cross the stile and turn right.*

2 *Turn right on the footpath marked Pitcroft Lane.*

6 *Follow the path through the farm buildings to the road and turn right.*

1 *Take the road past the war memorial, North Lane.*

Buriton

Buriton House

Cowhouse Farm

Old Ditcham Farm

Old Ditcham

7 *Where the road bends round to the left at the edge of the wood, go through the gate, following the sign marked right of way. Take the footpath which is furthest to the left of all the tracks – an obvious footpath rather than a vehicle track – and continue straight up the hill.*

Milky Way

11 *Cross the stile on the left, and follow the path across the field to the road and return to the start.*

Sunwood Farm

8 *Turn right at the road.*

10 *Where the road turns sharply to the left, take the path marked cart track to Buriton.*

9 *Turn right on the road immediately before the private road sign.*

Walk 27

STANSTED FOREST AND PARK

3½ miles (5½ km) Easy; muddy when wet

The walk begins at the village of Rowlands Castle, which lies to the east of the B2149, Horndean to Havant road. There is ample parking space either in the village streets or in the station car park. The walk lies entirely within or on the edge of Stansted forest. The starting place owes its name to a Norman motte and bailey castle, the remains of which can be seen to the south of the town. The forest itself was once the hunting ground of medieval kings, where Henry II had a hunting lodge built. Today, this is mixed woodland in which the different uses are indicated by the old names of the different sections: Firtree Piece; Oak Copse; and Hare Warren.

A A broad avenue leads from Rowland's Castle all the way up to Stansted House. Visitors to the great house in the eighteenth century could see all the way down from the dining room to the tall masts of the ships in Portsmouth Harbour. The avenue itself was once a good deal more impressive than it is today, for it was bordered by giant beech trees which sadly succumbed to disease in the 1970s. At the point where the avenue crosses the road, the entrance to Stansted Park is marked by an ornate gatehouse. From here, one would believe that one was looking along to an elegant Georgian manor but, in fact, the original was burned down in 1900 and then reconstructed. After this grand parade down towards Stansted House, the walk turns off into the woods, and remains a pleasant saunter through the trees all the way round and back to Rowland's Castle.

Over

0   1 mile

0   1 km

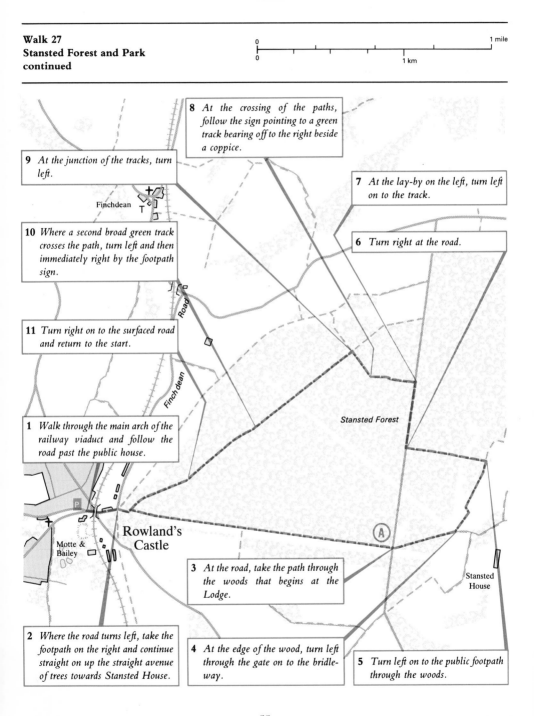

8 At the crossing of the paths, follow the sign pointing to a green track bearing off to the right beside a coppice.

9 At the junction of the tracks, turn left.

7 At the lay-by on the left, turn left on to the track.

Finchdean

10 Where a second broad green track crosses the path, turn left and then immediately right by the footpath sign.

6 Turn right at the road.

Road

11 Turn right on to the surfaced road and return to the start.

Finch dean

Stansted Forest

1 Walk through the main arch of the railway viaduct and follow the road past the public house.

Rowland's Castle

(A)

Motte & Bailey

Stansted House

3 At the road, take the path through the woods that begins at the Lodge.

2 Where the road turns left, take the footpath on the right and continue straight on up the straight avenue of trees towards Stansted House.

4 At the edge of the wood, turn left through the gate on to the bridle-way.

5 Turn left on to the public footpath through the woods.

Walk 28
EAST MEON

$3\frac{1}{2}$ miles ($5\frac{1}{2}$ km) Moderately difficult; often very muddy between points 9 and 10.

The walk starts at East Meon, which can be reached either by turning east off the A32 at West Meon or by turning south off the A272 at Langrish. There is parking in the village near the church. The appeal of the walk lies partly with the nature of the countryside. The clear ridge of the Downs, with its predominant east-west line and steep, north-facing scarp, has here come to an end and has been broken up into a series of isolated hills and undulating slopes.

Here, in fact, is a reversal of the usual pattern, with Park Hill appearing with its steepest slope to the south. So, although the walk has strong similarities to the other Downs' walks, there are subtle differences, notably in the way in which the little valleys break off at odd angles, while the open views across the Weald are replaced by views which now tend to be closed off by other hills. The other great appeal lies in the village of East Meon itself, where the walk starts.

A East Meon is a beautifully snug little village, crouching down into the narrow valley of the tiny River Meon, which has its source in springs a mile ($1\frac{1}{2}$ km) to the south. The clear waters of the river run right through the centre of the village, and give it a great deal of its charm. The place is dominated, however, by its church.

There has been a church at East Meon since Saxon times, but the present very grand building with its imposing tower and spire is primarily Norman. Its true glory, however, is inside – the font. It was brought here in the twelfth century, and is a solid block of marble carved by sculptors in Tournai in Flanders. The carvings tell the story of the Garden of Eden and the Fall, and are full of life and vigour, retaining all their original freshness.

The walk up the hillside behind the church gives a bird's-eye view of the village and reveals the ancient court house, the medieval manor of the Bishops of Winchester – and its presence explains the grandeur of the village church.

B Park Hill that rises above East Meon comes at the end of a long ridge that winds down from the north-east. It offers splendid walking on soft turf, with views across to the high point of the South Downs, Butser Hill. The most remarkable feature is a great hollow which seems to be scooped out of the face of the hill and is known as Vineyard Hole. Whether vines were grown here or not seems uncertain, but it is south facing and sheltered, so that it would seem the ideal spot. The eventual descent from the hill is through woodland that seems to cling precariously to the steep slope.

Over

Walk 28
East Meon
continued

0 ——————————————— 1 mile
0 ——————————————— 1 km

6 *Turn left at the corner of the hedge, following the path indicated by the yellow arrow.*

7 *At the bottom of the hollow, turn right on to the bridleway and continue on, ignoring the footpath sign.*

8 *Just beyond the line of pylons, the broad tracks diverge left and right, but continue straight on along the footpath down the steep gully through the woods.*

5 *At the end of the field, turn right.*

4 *At Park Farm, turn right along the path indicated by a sign next to the cottages.*

9 *At the foot of the hill, go through the gate and follow the line of the hedge.*

3 *At the wide stile, turn right and follow the direction indicated by the arrow around the curve of the hill.*

2 *Cross the stile and turn right up up the flight of steps.*

Park Farm

△ 205

Rookham Copse

Park Hill

(B)

Rookham Lodge Farm

Vineyard Hole

Barrow Hill

T

East Meon

P

Greenway Copse

A

1 *The walk starts at the church and goes through the churchyard past the west end of the church to a signposted footpath.*

10 *At the road, turn right and, after 70 yards (64 m), take the path to the left along an avenue of sycamores.*

13 *Turn left at the road and then right on to the footpath beside the stream, and continue on through an arch between the cottages past the Isaak Walton public house to the centre of the village.*

12 *Several paths meet in a small copse. Ignore the path heading back towards the right. The main path now divides: follow the branch to the right.*

11 *Ignore the prominent path turning to the left by a line of conifers.*

Walk 29

WEST MEON

4 miles (6½ km) Moderate

The walk begins at the village of West Meon, which is on the A32 1½ miles (2½ km) south of the junction with the A272. It covers an area of gently undulating agricultural land, dotted by woods and copses which, in its very gentleness, indicates that the Downs are coming to an end. If you think of the main range of the Downs as a long arm stretching west from Beachy Head, then here we have arrived at the hand, spreading out its fingers in different directions.

A West Meon village, like neighbouring East Meon, has been forced to squeeze itself into the narrow confines of the river valley. Here, however, there is even less free room for building, so that the buildings which cannot find space in the valley have to straggle up and down the enclosing hillsides. They are, as one comes to expect in this part of the country, a charming collection of cottages and small houses, some thatched, some roofed with rich, red tiles.

The most prominent building is the village church, something of a newcomer to the scene for it was built in the 1840s. It is a splendid example of the Gothic Revival at its most exuberant, and is the work of one of the founders of the movement, George Gilbert Scott, the elder. The churchyard contains the graves of some famous people, including that of Thomas Lord. He provided the ground on which the newly formed Marylebone Cricket Club first played its matches two centuries ago – it was to become the headquarters of cricket, and still bears his name, Lord's. Here also is the grave of the parents of the famous political writer, William Cobbett, who described this same country in his famous book, *Rural Rides*.

B Woodland and trees provide the dominant theme of this walk. After the long climb up from West Meon, with its wide vistas over the countryside, a magnificent avenue of beech trees leads you on to the woodland proper. Inevitably, parts of the woodland have been made over to conifers, but much of it remains as the older style of deciduous wood, with fine examples of that most typical of downland trees, the beech, mature oaks, and the real glory of the area, some splendid copper beeches.

Over

58

Walk 29
West Meon
continued

0   1 mile

0   1 km

7 *At the edge of the wood, turn left and follow the track along the side of the wood and straight on into the wood, keeping the plantation of newer trees on your right-hand side.*

6 *Turn left at the road.*

5 *Where the wide track swings round to the left to follow the edge of the field, continue straight on along a narrow path between fences through the wood.*

4 *Turn left at the road and then immediately right on to the sign-posted footpath.*

3 *Where two paths meet in a* T, *turn left.*

8 *At the end of the wood, turn left and follow the surfaced track past Bere Farm.*

9 *Turn left at the road.*

10 *Two hundred yards (180 m) along the wood, turn right on to the wide, stony path through the wood.*

11 *At the road, turn right to return to West Meon.*

1 *Start by turning up the minor road that runs between the war memorial and the Red Lion.*

2 *At the end of the houses, just before the end of a 30 mph zone, turn right up the footpath indicated by a wooden sign.*

Tumulus

(B)

Brockwood Copse

Westwood

Bere Farm

Meridell Farm

Lippen Wood

ROMAN VILLA
(site of)

West Meon

Laurel Dene

(A)

Warnford

Disused Railway

CORHAMPTON AND OLD WINCHESTER HILL

5 miles (8 km) Moderately difficult; quite strenuous between points 7 and 8

This walk begins at Corhampton on the A32. Turn west off the main road on to the B3035, Bishop's Waltham road, and then immediately right up a rough driveway to the Saxon church car park. This is a walk which offers tremendous variety of scenery, an equally varied type of footpath, and includes sites of historic interest that range through time from the Iron Age to the nineteenth century.

Scenically, you move out from the valley of the Meon to the top of a hill over 600 feet (180 m) above sea-level, passing through both woodland and pasture. The paths vary from conventional tracks across fields to a deep, tree-shaded lane and the track bed of an old railway. The history begins at the very start of the walk.

A Corhampton's Saxon church has no dedication to any saint, but is simply Corhampton church and so it has been since before the Norman Conquest. It remains basically a simple church of its period, though inevitably there have been alterations over the centuries. The most striking features are the wall paintings, which might be as old as the church, but are most likely to be twelfth century. The finest are in the chancel, and tell the story of St Swithun of Winchester, the narrative paintings being surrounded by purely decorative and heraldic devices.

There are interesting features outside. The sundial by the south porch is marked out to record the Saxon day, divided into eight instead of our familiar twelve units. The churchyard also boasts a yew tree of massive size and great antiquity. The village, which shades imperceptibly into Meonstoke, is a delightful spot through which the tiny River Meon gurgles. You can still see where it was once diverted to form a mill stream.

B The railway line which now provides the footpath for the next ½ mile (800 m) was once a branch line of the old London and South Western Railway, and originally ran from Basingstoke to Fareham, serving a dozen villages along the way. Like many another, it fell victim to the 'Beeching Axe' which lopped off branch lines in the 1950s.

Many of those are now finding a new use as walkways and cycle tracks. This section of our walk is, in fact, part of a much longer route that runs from Wickham for 9 miles (14½ km) to West Meon. Part of the charm of such routes lies in their memories of old steam engines puffing their slow, unhurried ways from halt to halt. But old railways have their own special environment. Many, as here, had trees planted alongside to function as windshields and boundary markers, and wild flowers flourish, untroubled by the sprays and croppings of agricultural land.

C Old Winchester Hill is crowned by the last of the great Iron Age hill forts that dot the tops of the downland hills on the journey from the east. It is a long, steady haul, partly up an open hillside and partly through woodland. The effort is richly rewarded.

The fort itself has an area of some 14 acres (5½ ha), enclosed by rampart and ditch. The earthworks are very impressive, with ramparts rising as high as 15 feet (4½ m) above the ditch, and with two clearly defined entrances at the eastern and western ends. The whole site is now a nature reserve and there are magnificent views over rich, downland countryside. The view to the north is particularly pleasing, where a deep valley sweeps away from the hill, one flank covered by woodland flecked with the dark green of fine yew trees.

Over

0   1 mile
0   1 km

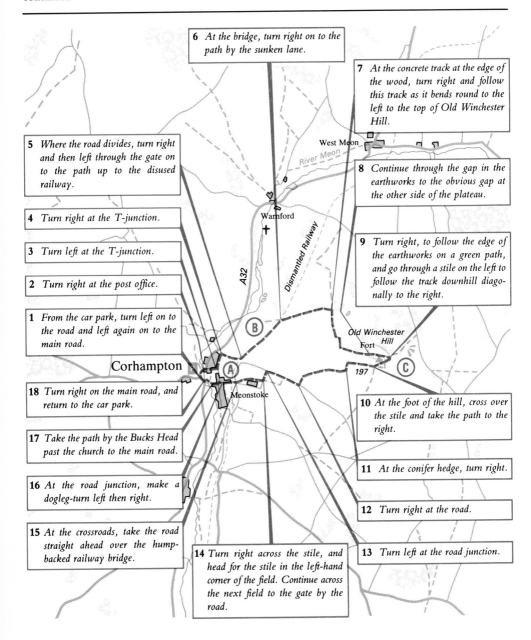

6 *At the bridge, turn right on to the path by the sunken lane.*

7 *At the concrete track at the edge of the wood, turn right and follow this track as it bends round to the left to the top of Old Winchester Hill.*

5 *Where the road divides, turn right and then left through the gate on to the path up to the disused railway.*

8 *Continue through the gap in the earthworks to the obvious gap at the other side of the plateau.*

4 *Turn right at the T-junction.*

9 *Turn right, to follow the edge of the earthworks on a green path, and go through a stile on the left to follow the track downhill diagonally to the right.*

3 *Turn left at the T-junction.*

2 *Turn right at the post office.*

1 *From the car park, turn left on to the road and left again on to the main road.*

18 *Turn right on the main road, and return to the car park.*

10 *At the foot of the hill, cross over the stile and take the path to the right.*

17 *Take the path by the Bucks Head past the church to the main road.*

11 *At the conifer hedge, turn right.*

16 *At the road junction, make a dogleg-turn left then right.*

12 *Turn right at the road.*

15 *At the crossroads, take the road straight ahead over the hump-backed railway bridge.*

14 *Turn right across the stile, and head for the stile in the left-hand corner of the field. Continue across the next field to the gate by the road.*

13 *Turn left at the road junction.*

West Meon

River Meon

Warnford

A32

Dismantled Railway

Corhampton

Meonstoke

B

A

C

Old Winchester Hill

Fort

197

Walk 31

CHERITON

3 miles (4¾ km) Easy

The walk begins at Cheriton which lies on the B3046 between New Alresford on the A31 and New Cheriton on the A272. Park by the village green. This is a gentle walk on the very edge of the downland, an area brought to an end by the River Itchen, which runs down from the hills to the south of the village, turns sharply west, and then swings south again through Winchester to the sea. It is largely a peaceful, agricultural landscape of fields and meadows, though it has seen its moments of drama, for there was a Civil War battle fought in the area between Cheriton village and Cheriton Wood in 1644.

A Cheriton village is a model of what an English village should be, the kind of place that exiles dream about in reveries of rural England. There are no striking individual features, but a happy combination of elements. Houses in a plain vernacular, using local materials, sit comfortably round the village green. The Itchen, here little more than a stream, runs through the green while ducks waddle over the grass or float on the clear water. There are memories of great antiquity, for the village church stands on a prehistoric mound. It all adds up to the sort of picture that has many times earned Cheriton the title of Best Kept Village in Hampshire.

B The walk out from Cheriton follows the line of the Itchen through rich, lush watermeadows. The river itself is lined with trees, through which the water is glimpsed as an occasional sparkle, while the meadows themselves are a delight, with long grasses dotted with flowers. This section ends at Cheriton mill. It is a simple, but attractive red-brick building with a tiled roof, with an equally attractive mill house alongside. The mill stream and pond are silted and overgrown but still distinctive, while the river a few yards to the east flows quietly on its way, its banks bright with yellow flags.

C At this point on the walk, one could say that three quite distinct landscapes meet. The way itself passes through a deep, sunken lane, part of a complex pattern of paths and tracks which have been in use since medieval times and probably earlier. This path links Cheriton to Cheriton Wood, which itself overlies an ancient field system. All around, you can see the gentle swellings of old grazing land, and this same path would have been used by shepherds bringing their flocks down to the Itchen valley.

In the field immediately to the north of the track is the prominent hump of a Neolithic long barrow or burial mound. Immediately south, however, there is a very different view. This is the formal parkland of Hinton Ampner House. The idea is very much that of the eighteenth century, but the trees chosen for their contrasting beauties – lime, chestnut, maple, and Turkey oak – have mainly been planted in this century. So different generations have added their own distinctive features to this lovely landscape.

Over

0   1 mile

0   1 km

4 *Pass through a garden to the road and turn right, crossing the main road to follow the green lane straight ahead.*

5 *At the track junction, turn right, ignoring the arrows pointing to the Wayfarers Walk.*

6 *Where the track divides, take the left-hand fork.*

River Itchen

B3046

Ⓑ Cheriton Mill

3 *Climb over the stile on the right, marked with an arrow and the letters WW (Wayfarers Walk), and follow the path beside the stream.*

North End

Cheriton

Long Barrow

Ⓒ

2 *Turn left down Hillhouses Lane beside the high brick wall.*

Ⓐ

P

Hinton Marsh

1 *From the war memorial, walk along the road by the village green keeping the green on the right-hand side.*

8 *Turn right at the road to return to Cheriton.*

7 *Turn right at the footpath crossing, by a prominent group of trees, and follow the broad track.*

Walk 32

CHEESEFOOT HEAD AND FAWLEY DOWN

0   ½ mile
0   ½ km

3½ miles (5½ km) Easy

The walk begins at Cheesefoot Head. The car park is on the A272, 1 mile (1½ km) from the junction with the A31, and is marked by a prominent clump of trees to the north of the road. Fawley Down marks the western limit of the South Downs, but the countryside still has the essential downland character of swelling hills and swooping valleys, where paths along the high ground offer wide vistas while the deep, sunken lanes provide hedgerows bright with flowers and busy with birds and insects. A word of caution is necessary, however, for this walk: the area to the west is used for military exercises, so it is important to keep to the pathway while walking south. A red flag flies when exercises are in progress.

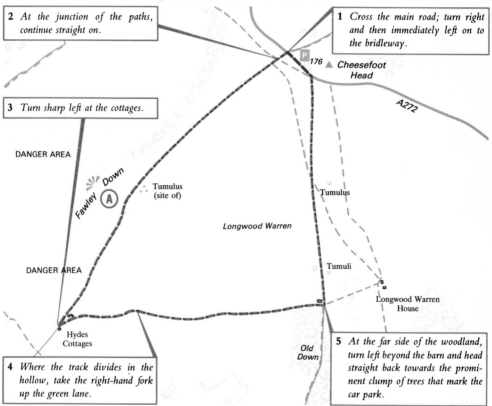

2 *At the junction of the paths, continue straight on.*

1 *Cross the main road; turn right and then immediately left on to the bridleway.*

176 ▲ Cheesefoot Head

A272

3 *Turn sharp left at the cottages.*

DANGER AREA

Fawley Down (A)

Tumulus (site of)

Tumulus

Longwood Warren

DANGER AREA

Tumuli

Longwood Warren House

Hydes Cottages

Old Down

4 *Where the track divides in the hollow, take the right-hand fork up the green lane.*

5 *At the far side of the woodland, turn left beyond the barn and head straight back towards the prominent clump of trees that mark the car park.*

A This very open section of the walk provides excellent views across the rough ground to the east towards the valley of the Itchen and the ancient city of Winchester. The road to the west of Fawley Down lies along the route of the old Roman road from Winchester to Wickham, and is unusual in that it turns through a right-angle by Beacon Hill.

BARTHOLOMEW WALKS SERIES

Designed to meet the requirements of both experienced and inexperienced walkers, the guides in this series are ideal for anyone who enjoys exploring on foot. They describe the best routes across our greatest walking country from Inverness to the New Forest and Cork & Kerry.

● In each guide, there are at least 30 carefully chosen, easy-to-follow walks over rights of way, with detailed route descriptions accompanying special maps.

● Country walks are graded according to distance and terrain and start from a convenient parking area. The route always returns to the car park, usually by a circular walk and, where appropriate, access by public transport is also possible.

● Notes on local history, geography and wildlife add interest to the walks and the unique notebook format is especially easy to use.

WALK CORK & KERRY
0 7028 0949 7 £4·95

WALK THE CORNISH COASTAL PATH
A special format step-by-step guide to the entire length of the Cornish Coastal Path (Marsland Mouth - Cremyll).
0 7028 0902 0 £4·99

WALK THE COTSWOLDS
0 7028 0908 X £4·99

WALK THE DALES
0 7028 0800 8 £4·99

MORE WALKS IN THE DALES
0 7028 0948 9 £4·95

YORKSHIRE DALES VISITOR'S PACK
Containing a copy of *Walk the Dales* and a folded 1 inch map of the Yorkshire Dales in a clear, plastic carrying wallet.
0 7028 0932 2 £6·99

WALK DARTMOOR
0 7028 0688 9 £3·95

WALK DEVON & CORNWALL
0 7028 1283 8 £4·99

WALK DORSET & HARDY'S WESSEX
0 7028 0906 3 £3·95

WALK EDINBURGH & THE PENTLANDS
0 7028 1280 3 £4·99

WALK EXMOOR & THE QUANTOCKS
0 7028 0910 1 £3·95

WALK HERTS & BUCKS
0 7028 0953 5 £4·95

WALK THE ISLE OF WIGHT
0 7028 1279 X £4·99

WALK THE LAKES
0 7028 8111 2 £4·99

MORE WALKS IN THE LAKES
0 7028 0819 9 £4·99

LAKE DISTRICT WALKING PACK
Containing a copy of *Walk the Lakes* and a folded 1 inch map of the Lake District in a clear, plastic carrying wallet.
0 7028 0876 8 £6·99

WALK LOCH LOMOND & THE TROSSACHS
0 7028 0744 3 £4·99

BARTHOLOMEW WALKS SERIES (Contd)

WALK OBAN, MULL & LOCHABER
0 7028 0801 6 £3·95

WALK THE PEAK DISTRICT
0 7028 0710 9 £4·99

MORE WALKS IN THE PEAK DISTRICT
0 7028 0951 9 £4·95

WALK PERTHSHIRE
0 7028 0766 4 £3·95

WALK LOCH NESS & THE RIVER SPEY
0 7028 0787 7 £3·95

**WALK ROYAL DEESIDE
& NORTH EAST SCOTLAND**
0 7028 0898 9 £3·95

WALK LOTHIAN, THE BORDERS & FIFE
0 7028 0803 2 £3·95

WALK THE NEW FOREST
0 7028 0810 5 £4·99

WALK SNOWDONIA & NORTH WALES
0 7028 0804 0 £3·95

WALK THE NORTH DOWNS
0 7028 0742 7 £4·99

WALK THE SOUTH DOWNS
0 7028 0811 3 £4·99

WALK THE NORTH YORK MOORS
0 7028 0743 5 £4·99

WALK THE SOUTH PENNINES
0 7028 0955 1 £4·95

WALK NORTHUMBRIA
0 7028 0959 4 £4·95

NORTHUMBRIA WALKING PACK
Containing a copy of *Walk Northumbria* and a folded
copy of the Northumberland & Durham Leisure
Map in a clear, plastic carrying wallet.
0 7028 1216 1 £6·99

**WALK SOUTH WALES
& THE WYE VALLEY**
0 7028 0904 7 £3·95

WALK SOUTH WEST SCOTLAND
0 7028 0900 4 £3·95

Guides in this series may be purchased from good bookshops. In the event of difficulty copies may be obtained by post.
Please send your order with your remittance to
**BARTHOLOMEW BOOKSERVICE BY POST,
PO BOX 29, DOUGLAS, ISLE OF MAN, BRITISH ISLES.**

NAME _____

ADDRESS _____

_____

Please enclose a cheque or postal order made out to 'Bartholomew' for the amount due and allow 25 pence per book
postage & packing fee up to a maximum of £3.00.
While every effort is made to keep prices low, it is sometimes necessary to increase cover prices at short notice.
Bartholomew reserves the right to show new retail prices on covers which may differ from those previously advertised in
the text or elsewhere.